HAMLYN'S ALL-COLOUR BOOK OF

Casserole Cookery

HAMLYN

LONDON · NEW YORK · SYDNEY · TORONTO

Acknowledgements
Recipes created by Julia Roles
Photography by John Lee
Cover picture by Iain Reid
Artwork by John Scott Martin
China kindly loaned by Denby Tableware Limited,
Royal Doulton Tableware Limited and Pointerware
(UK) Limited

Published by
The Hamlyn Publishing Group Limited
London · New York · Sydney · Toronto
Astronaut House, Feltham, Middlesex, England
ISBN 0 600 31941 5

Printed in England by Jarrold and Sons Limited, Norwich

Contents

Introduction

Casseroles may be made with fish, beef, lamb, pork, veal, offal, poultry, game, vegetables or fruit as the main ingredient. Recipes for all these are given in this book.

The *liquid* used in casseroles may be stock, red or white wine, beer, dry cider or canned tomatoes. Do not add too much liquid as there is only a little lost during the cooking process. If liked a casserole may be *thickened* at the end of the cooking time with blended cornflour or beurre manié – equal quantities of butter and flour made into a paste which is whisked into the casserole a little at a time. Alternatively, flour may be added during the preparation.

How to prepare meat, poultry and game casseroles

In order to obtain a good flavour to the finished dish it is important to sauté (or seal) the meat or poultry first so that the flavour and juices do not escape during the cooking. This is done by lightly frying the prepared pieces or joint of meat in a little fat until browned on all sides. After the meat has been sautéed and removed to the casserole dish the vegetables may also be sautéed, but this is not essential. Add the flour (if used at this stage) and allow it to colour slightly, then gradually stir in the liquid scraping up all the juices and then pour over the meat. Add any additional ingredients, cover the dish and cook either on a low heat on top of the cooker or in a slow oven. When using the top of the cooker, it is necessary to stir the casserole from time to time.

Cookware for casseroles

You may cook a casserole in a covered *saucepan* on top of the cooker, in which case it is best to do the initial frying in a shallow pan and then transfer the ingredients to the saucepan. *Ovenproof dishes* may be used and with these the initial frying is also carried out in a shallow pan. *Flameproof casseroles* usually made from enamel or enamel-coated cast iron are excellent for casseroles as the initial frying can be done in batches on top of the cooker in the same dish thus cutting down on washing-up.

Freezing casseroles

All freezer owners will discover how well most casseroles freeze and how easy it is to make double the quantity and freeze half for future use. Avoid over-seasoning casseroles to be frozen and omit the garlic which can be added at the reheating stage. Do not include potatoes, rice or pasta which will lose texture during freezing. It is best to allow a casserole to cool and freeze it in a rigid container or foil bag, leaving a small headspace for the expansion of liquid on freezing. If you want to use the same dish for reheating, line it with freezer foil and ladle in the cooled casserole. Form the foil into a parcel and freeze in the dish. When solid remove the package from the dish and seal the parcel. To reheat, unwrap and return the frozen shape to the dish.

Useful facts and figures

Notes on metrication

In this book quantities are given in metric, imperial and American measures. Exact conversion from imperial to metric measures does not usually give very convenient working quantities and so the metric measures have been rounded off into units of 25 grams. The table below shows the recommended equivalents.

Ounces	Approx. g to nearest whole figure	Recommended conversion to nearest unit of 25
1	28	25
2	57	50
3	85	75
4	113	100
5	142	150
6	170	175
7	198	200
8	227	225
9	255	250
10	283	275
11	312	300
12	340	350
13	368	375
14	397	400
15	425	425
16 (1 lb)	454	450
17	482	475
18	510	500
19	539	550
20	567	575

Note: When converting quantities over 20 oz first add the appropriate figures in the centre column, then adjust to the nearest unit of 25. As a general guide, 1 kg (1000 g) equals 2.2 lb or about 2 lb 3 oz. Quantities of such ingredients as vegetables, fruit, meat and fish which are not critical are rounded off to the nearest quarter of a kg as this is how they are likely to be purchased.

Liquid measures The millilitre has been used in this book and the following tables gives a few examples:

Imperial	Approx. ml to nearest whole figure	Recommended ml
¼ pint	142	150 ml
½ pint	283	300 ml
¾ pint	425	450 ml
1 pint	567	600 ml
1½ pints	851	900 ml
1¾ pints	992	1000 ml (1 litre)

Note: For quantities of 1¾ pints and over we have used litres and fractions of a litre.

Spoon measures All spoon measures given in this book are level.

Can sizes At present, cans are marked with the exact (usually to the nearest whole number) metric equivalent of the imperial weight of the contents, so we have followed this practice when giving can sizes.

Oven temperatures
The table below gives recommended equivalents.

	°F	°C	Gas Mark
Very cool	225	110	¼
	250	120	½
Cool	275	140	1
	300	150	2
Moderate	325	160	3
	350	180	4
Moderately hot	375	190	5
	400	200	6
Hot	425	220	7
	450	230	8
Very hot	475	240	9

Note: When making any of the recipes in this book, only follow one set of measures as they are not interchangeable.

Notes for American users
Although the recipes in this book give American measures, the lists below give some equivalents or substitutes for terms and commodities which may be unfamiliar to American readers.

Equipment and terms
BRITISH/AMERICAN

cocktail stick/toothpick
frying pan/skillet
greaseproof paper/waxed paper
grill/broil
kitchen paper/paper towels
liquidise/blend

mince/grind
packet/package
polythene/plastic
roasting tin/roasting pan
stoned/pitted

Ingredients
BRITISH/AMERICAN

aubergine/eggplant
beetroot/beet
belly of pork/salt pork
black cherries/Bing cherries
black olives/ripe olives
boiling chicken/stewing chicken
chicory/Belgian endive
chilli/chili
chipolatas/link sausages
chipped potatoes/French fries
cornflour/cornstarch
courgette/zucchini
double cream/heavy cream
essence/extract
fillet/tenderloin
gelatine/gelatin
gherkin/sweet dill pickle
ham/cured or smoked ham
hard-boiled egg/hardcooked egg
haricot beans/navy beans
icing sugar/confectioners' sugar

ketchup/catsup
lard/shortening
marrow/squash
minced beef/ground beef
natural yogurt/unflavored yogurt
offal/variety meats
pig's liver/pork liver
plain flour/all-purpose flour
puff pastry/puff paste
self-raising flour/self-rising flour
shortcrust pastry/basic pie dough
single cream/light cream
soured cream/sour cream
spring onions/scallions
streaky bacon rashers/bacon slices
sultanas/seedless white raisins
sweetcorn/corn kernels
tomato purée/tomato paste
topside of beef/top round of beef
unsalted butter/sweet butter
veal escalopes/veal scallops

Note: The British and Australian pint is 20 fluid ounces as opposed to the American pint which is 16 fluid ounces.

Notes for Australian users
Ingredients in this book are given in cup, metric and imperial measures. In Australia the American 8-oz measuring cup is used in conjunction with the imperial pint of 20 fluid ounces. It is most important to remember that the Australian tablespoon differs from both the British and American tablespoons; the table below gives a comparison between the standard tablespoons used in the three countries. The British standard tablespoon holds 17.7 millilitres, the American 14.2 millilitres, and the Australian 20 millilitres. A teaspoon holds approximately 5 millilitres in all three countries.

British	American	Australian
1 teaspoon	1 teaspoon	1 teaspoon
1 tablespoon	1 tablespoon	1 tablespoon
2 tablespoons	3 tablespoons	2 tablespoons
3½ tablespoons	4 tablespoons	3 tablespoons
4 tablespoons	5 tablespoons	3½ tablespoons

Fish casseroles

Many people forget that fish can be cooked in a casserole – in fact it is an ideal method because the full flavour is retained. The preparation is quick and easy as it is not necessary to sauté the fish prior to cooking it. When possible use dry white wine as some or all of the cooking liquid – it greatly enhances the flavour of the finished dish. Use parsley, watercress, anchovy fillets, olives or lemon slices as a garnish.

Cod à la provençale

METRIC/IMPERIAL/AMERICAN
0.5 kg/1 lb/2 cups tomatoes, peeled and chopped
1 rosemary sprig, chopped
2 thyme sprigs, chopped
salt and pepper
2 tablespoons/2 tablespoons/3 tablespoons white wine or
    water
3 shallots, chopped
2 cloves garlic, crushed
2 tablespoons/2 tablespoons/3 tablespoons olive oil
0.75 kg/1½ lb/1½ lb cod fillets
few drops anchovy essence (optional)
chopped parsley to garnish

Place the tomatoes in a saucepan with the herbs, seasoning and wine or water. Bring to the boil, then cover and simmer gently for about 15 minutes until soft and pulpy.

Meanwhile, sauté the shallots and garlic in the olive oil until softened.

Lay the fish in the bottom of a casserole and season lightly. Arrange the shallots on top. Add a few drops of anchovy essence to the tomato sauce, if liked, and pour over the fish. Cover and cook in a moderate oven (180°C, 350°F, Gas Mark 4) for 30 minutes. Garnish with chopped parsley and serve with French bread.

Serves 4

Mackerel in mustard sauce

METRIC/IMPERIAL/AMERICAN
4 medium mackerel or herrings
salt and freshly ground pepper
1 tablespoon cornflour
3–4 tablespoons/3–4 tablespoons/4–5 tablespoons made
  mustard
4 tablespoons/4 tablespoons/⅓ cup white wine
1 tablespoon lemon juice
GARNISH:
watercress sprigs
tomato waterlilies

Cut the heads and tails off the fish, gut them and remove the backbones. Lay the fish, skin side down, in a casserole, season with salt and pepper. Mix together the cornflour and mustard, then gradually blend in the wine and lemon juice.

Pour the sauce over the fish, cover and cook in a moderate oven (160°C, 325°F, Gas Mark 3) for 30 minutes. Garnish with watercress and tomato waterlilies, serve with crusty brown bread.

Serves 4

Curried haddock

METRIC/IMPERIAL/AMERICAN
0.75 kg/1½ lb/1½ lb haddock fillets
50 g/2 oz/¼ cup butter
2 onions, finely chopped
1 clove garlic, crushed
1 apple, peeled and sliced
1–1½ tablespoons curry powder
1 tablespoon flour
300 ml/½ pint/1¼ cups chicken stock
225 g/8 oz/1 cup tomatoes, peeled and chopped
2 tablespoons/2 tablespoons/3 tablespoons tomato purée
1 tablespoon lemon juice
1 (2.5-cm/1-inch/1-inch) piece root ginger, chopped
salt and pepper
lemon wedges and watercress sprigs to garnish

Cut the fish into 2.5-cm/1-inch pieces and place in a casserole. Melt the butter in a saucepan and sauté the onions and garlic for 3 minutes. Add the apple and cook for 2 minutes. Mix together the curry powder and flour and sprinkle into the pan. Cook, stirring, for 2 minutes. Remove from the heat and stir in the stock, tomatoes, tomato purée, lemon juice, ginger and seasoning. Bring to the boil, stirring, then pour over the fish. Mix well, cover and place in a moderate oven (160°C, 325°F, Gas Mark 3) for 30 minutes. Garnish and serve with boiled rice.

Serves 4

Sole with prawns

METRIC/IMPERIAL/AMERICAN
0.5 kg/1 lb/1 lb sole fillets
flour for coating
3 tablespoons/3 tablespoons/¼ cup olive oil
2 onions, finely chopped
2 cloves garlic, crushed
225 g/8 oz/½ lb frozen prawns, thawed
3 tomatoes, peeled and roughly chopped
1 teaspoon chopped fresh thyme
½ teaspoon cayenne pepper
300 ml/½ pint/1¼ cups white wine
2 tablespoons/2 tablespoons/3 tablespoons tomato purée
1 tablespoon lemon juice
salt and pepper
1 egg yolk
3 tablespoons/3 tablespoons/¼ cup cream
slices of lemon and parsley sprig to garnish

Cut the sole into pieces and coat with flour. Heat the oil in a flameproof casserole and sauté the onions and garlic for 2–3 minutes. Add the prawns and sole and continue cooking until the onion is soft. Stir in the tomatoes, thyme, cayenne, white wine, tomato purée and lemon juice. Season. Bring to the boil, then cover and simmer for 15–20 minutes, or cook in a moderate oven (160°C, 325°F, Gas Mark 3). Beat together the egg yolk and cream and stir into the wine sauce, off the heat. Warm through only. Garnish and serve with boiled rice.

Serves 6

Sole véronique

METRIC/IMPERIAL/AMERICAN
1 small onion, finely chopped
15 g/½ oz/1 tablespoon butter
0.75 kg/1½ lb/1½ lb sole or plaice fillets
salt and pepper
juice of ½ lemon
150 ml/¼ pint/⅔ cup white wine
1 bay leaf
175 g/6 oz/6 oz white grapes, peeled and deseeded
25 g/1 oz/2 tablespoons butter
25 g/1 oz/¼ cup flour
150 ml/¼ pint/⅔ cup double cream

Sprinkle the onion over the bottom of a buttered casserole. Fold the sole fillets in half and place on top of the onion. Season and add the lemon juice, wine, bay leaf and enough water to cover. Cover and cook in a moderate oven (180°C, 350°F, Gas Mark 4) for 15 minutes. Reserve a few grapes for garnishing and add the remaining grapes to the dish. Return to the oven to heat. Remove the fish and grapes and keep warm. Discard bay leaf.

Melt the butter in a saucepan, blend in the flour and cook for 1 minute. Remove from the heat and strain in the cooking liquid, made up to 300 ml/½ pint/1¼ cups with extra wine or water. Bring to the boil, stirring. Cook until thick. Remove from the heat and add the cream. Heat through only.

Return the fish and grapes to the casserole or arrange on a serving dish, and pour the sauce over. Garnish with watercress.

Serves 4

Spicy fish and tomato bake

METRIC/IMPERIAL/AMERICAN
4 cod steaks
¼ teaspoon ground turmeric
salt and pepper
1 fresh chilli, roughly chopped
½ teaspoon cumin seeds
1 clove garlic
4 large tomatoes, peeled and halved
6 cloves
6 peppercorns
1 onion, finely chopped
2 tablespoons/2 tablespoons/3 tablespoons oil
2 tablespoons/2 tablespoons/3 tablespoons wine vinegar
3 eggs
watercress sprig to garnish

Rub the fish with the turmeric and salt. Grind the chilli, cumin seeds and garlic to a paste. Cook the tomatoes until soft with 150 ml/¼ pint/⅔ cup water, cloves and peppercorns; sieve.

Sauté the onion in the oil until golden. Add the chilli paste and sauté for 2–3 minutes, stirring. Add the fish, puréed tomatoes, vinegar and seasoning. Simmer for 10 minutes then cool slightly. Transfer the fish to an ovenproof dish.

Separate 2 eggs and beat the whites until stiff. Add the beaten yolks. Stir the remaining beaten egg into the tomato sauce, off the heat. Pour over the fish. Spread the beaten egg mixture on top, bake in the oven (180°C, 350°F, Gas Mark 4) for 20 minutes.

Serves 4

Plaice Seville

METRIC/IMPERIAL/AMERICAN
0.75 kg/1½ lb/1½ lb plaice fillets
2 tablespoons/2 tablespoons/3 tablespoons lemon juice
1 teaspoon salt
2 oranges
100 g/4 oz/1 cup mushrooms, chopped (optional)
1 (250-g/8¾-oz/8¾-oz) can crushed pineapple or pineapple tidbits, drained
100 g/4 oz/¼ lb grapes, skinned and deseeded
½ teaspoon chilli powder
150 ml/¼ pint/⅔ cup single cream
watercress sprig to garnish

Marinate the fish for 15 minutes in the lemon juice and salt. Drain, fold the fillets and place in a casserole. Peel the oranges, remove all pith and divide into segments. Mix with the remaining ingredients and spoon over the fish. Cover and cook in a moderate oven (160°C, 325°F, Gas Mark 3) for 20–30 minutes or until tender. Garnish with watercress.

Serves 4

Halibut with cheesy topping

METRIC/IMPERIAL/AMERICAN
75 g/3 oz/6 tablespoons butter
100 g/4 oz/1 cup mushrooms, sliced
4 shallots, finely chopped
1 clove garlic, crushed
6 (175-g/6-oz/6-oz) halibut steaks
300 ml/½ pint/1¼ cups dry white wine
150 ml/¼ pint/⅔ cup water
1 bay leaf
25 g/1 oz/¼ cup flour
150 ml/¼ pint/⅔ cup double cream
50 g/2 oz/½ cup cheese, grated
25 g/1 oz/½ cup fresh breadcrumbs
slices of tomato to garnish

Melt two-thirds of the butter in a flameproof casserole. Add the mushrooms, shallots and garlic and sauté until soft. Lay the fish steaks on top. Pour over the wine and water mixed, and the bay leaf. Cover and cook in a moderate oven (180°C, 350°F, Gas Mark 4) for 20 minutes.

Measure 300 ml/½ pint/1¼ cups of the strained cooking liquor. Melt the remaining butter and stir in the flour. Cook for 1 minute then blend in the measured fish stock. Bring to the boil, stirring. Remove from the heat, add the cream and adjust seasoning. Pour over the fish and sprinkle with the cheese and breadcrumbs. Return to the oven for 10 minutes. Garnish.

Serves 6

Haddock with shellfish in béchamel sauce

METRIC/IMPERIAL/AMERICAN
600 ml/1 pint/2½ cups milk
2 onions
12 peppercorns
pinch nutmeg
0.75 kg/1½ lb/1½ lb haddock fillets
65 g/2½ oz/½ cup plus 2 tablespoons flour
100 g/4 oz/½ cup butter
1 green pepper, deseeded and chopped
salt and pepper
100 g/4 oz/¼ lb frozen prawns, thawed
chopped parsley to garnish

Bring the milk with 1 onion, peppercorns and nutmeg to the boil. Remove from the heat and infuse for 30 minutes.

Meanwhile, cut the haddock into pieces and coat with 25 g/1 oz/¼ cup flour. Melt half the butter and sauté the fish until coloured. Transfer to a casserole. Slice the second onion and sauté with the pepper in the butter. Add to the fish.

Melt the remaining butter in a pan and stir in the remaining flour. Cook for 1 minute, remove from the heat and strain in the hot milk. Mix well and, stirring, bring to the boil and cook until thickened. Season and add the prawns. Pour on to the haddock and vegetables. Cover and cook in a moderate oven (180°C, 350°F, Gas Mark 4) for 15–20 minutes. Garnish.

Serves 6–8

Savoury topped fish

METRIC/IMPERIAL/AMERICAN
4 (175-g/6-oz/6-oz) white fish fillets (cod, whiting or
  haddock)
50 g/2 oz/¼ cup butter, melted
salt and pepper
4 tomatoes, sliced
2 shallots, finely chopped
1 small green pepper, deseeded and chopped
25 g/1 oz/½ cup fresh white breadcrumbs
50 g/2 oz/½ cup Cheddar cheese, grated
½ teaspoon Worcestershire sauce
1 teaspoon mixed dried herbs
1 lemon or orange
GARNISH:
twist of lemon or orange
parsley sprig

Place the fish in a well-greased casserole and spoon over half the
melted butter. Season and arrange the tomato slices on top.
  Sauté the shallots and green pepper in the remaining butter
until softened. Mix in the breadcrumbs, cheese, Worcestershire
sauce, herbs and the juice and grated rind of the lemon or
orange. Season to taste and spread over the fish and tomatoes.
Bake in a moderate oven (180°C, 350°F, Gas Mark 4) for 30
minutes. Garnish with a twist of lemon or orange and a sprig of
parsley. Serve with minted peas and new potatoes.

Serves 4

Smoked haddock à la russe

METRIC/IMPERIAL/AMERICAN
0.75 kg/1½ lb/1½ lb smoked haddock fillets
300 ml/½ pint/1¼ cups white wine
freshly ground black pepper and salt
25 g/1 oz/2 tablespoons butter
25 g/1 oz/¼ cup flour
½ small green pepper, deseeded and chopped
150 ml/¼ pint/⅔ cup soured cream
GARNISH:
croûtes of bread cut into star shapes
parsley sprig

Place the haddock in a large frying pan and add the wine. Add
enough water to cover. Season with pepper. Bring to the boil,
skim the surface then lower the heat and simmer for 5 minutes.
Remove the fish, drain reserving the cooking liquor, and cut
into squares. Place in a casserole.
  Melt the butter in a saucepan and stir in the flour. Cook,
stirring, for 1 minute then remove from the heat and gradually
blend in 300 ml/½ pint/1¼ cups of the strained cooking liquor.
Return to the heat and bring to the boil, stirring continuously.
When the sauce is thick and glossy, add the chopped pepper and
season to taste. Pour the sauce over the fish and mix well. Cover
and cook in a moderate oven (180°C, 350°F, Gas Mark 4) for 20
minutes. Stir in the soured cream and return to the oven to heat
through. Garnish and serve with buttered new potatoes.

Serves 4–6

Beef casseroles

Beef casseroles are always popular and they need never become boring. The changes can be rung by the addition of herbs and different vegetables; stock, wine or ale may be part or all of the cooking liquid. The cuts of beef to choose for casseroles range from chuck, skirt and minced beef to joints of brisket and topside which may be pot-roasted.

Beef Brazilian style

METRIC/IMPERIAL/AMERICAN
1 kg/2 lb/2 lb skirt steak
3 tablespoons/3 tablespoons/$\frac{1}{4}$ cup oil
3 onions, sliced into rings
1 clove garlic, crushed
25 g/1 oz/$\frac{1}{4}$ cup flour
150 ml/$\frac{1}{4}$ pint/$\frac{2}{3}$ cup black coffee (1$\frac{1}{2}$–2 teaspoons instant coffee dissolved in 150 ml/$\frac{1}{4}$ pint/$\frac{2}{3}$ cup boiling water)
150 ml/$\frac{1}{4}$ pint/$\frac{2}{3}$ cup beef stock or red wine
1 (396-g/14-oz/14-oz) can tomatoes
salt and pepper
pinch nutmeg
2 teaspoons soft brown sugar

Cut the meat into strips and fry quickly in the oil. Lower the heat and add the onions and garlic. Cook until softened. Sprinkle in the flour and continue to cook, stirring, for a further minute. Gradually mix in the coffee and stock or wine, then add the tomatoes. Season with salt, pepper, nutmeg and the soft brown sugar. Bring to simmering point, cover and cook in a moderate oven (160°C, 325°F, Gas Mark 3) for 2 hours. Serve with buttered noodles and a green salad.

Serves 4

Madras beef

METRIC/IMPERIAL/AMERICAN
0.75 kg/1½ lb/1½ lb chuck steak
freshly ground black pepper and salt
50 g/2 oz/½ cup flour
50 g/2 oz/¼ cup ghee or butter
3 onions, chopped
2 cloves garlic, crushed
1 teaspoon ground coriander
1 teaspoon ground cloves
½–1 teaspoon ground cinnamon
1 teaspoon ground turmeric
2 teaspoons chilli powder
1 teaspoon ground ginger
½ teaspoon ground cardamom
1 teaspoon cumin seeds
1 bay leaf
600 ml/1 pint/2½ cups beef stock
juice of ½ lemon

Cut the beef into pieces and coat with black pepper and half the
flour. Melt the ghee or butter in a flameproof casserole and fry
the meat until brown. Remove. Add the onions and garlic and
sauté until softened. Sprinkle in the spices and the flour and mix
well. Cook for 2 minutes then remove from the heat and stir in
the stock and lemon juice. Bring to the boil, stirring. Reduce the
heat, return the meat and adjust seasoning. Cover and cook in a
moderate oven (160°C, 325°F, Gas Mark 3) for 2–2½ hours.

Serves 4

Chilli con carne

METRIC/IMPERIAL/AMERICAN
2 onions, chopped
1 red or green pepper, deseeded and chopped
2 tablespoons/2 tablespoons/3 tablespoons corn oil
0.75 kg/1½ lb/1½ lb lean minced beef
1 tablespoon tomato purée
few drops Tabasco sauce
1–2 tablespoons chilli powder or 1 fresh chilli, finely
    chopped
1 (425-g/15-oz/15-oz) can red kidney beans, drained
1 (425-g/15-oz/15-oz) can tomatoes
salt and pepper
pinch cayenne pepper

In a flameproof casserole, fry the onions and pepper in the oil
until softened. Add the meat and continue frying, stirring
occasionally, until browned. Blend in the tomato purée,
Tabasco sauce, chilli powder or fresh chilli, drained kidney
beans and tomatoes with their juice. Season to taste with salt,
pepper and cayenne. Cover and cook on top of the cooker or in
a moderate oven (160°C, 325°F, Gas Mark 3) for 45 minutes–
1 hour. Serve with boiled rice.

Serves 4

Pot-au-feu

METRIC/IMPERIAL/AMERICAN
1.25 kg/2½ lb/2½ lb topside
3 litres/5¼ pints/6½ pints beef stock
salt and pepper
0.5 kg/1 lb/1 lb carrots, sliced
2 large onions, quartered
bouquet garni
2 turnips, quartered
4 leeks
2–3 sticks celery
1 small cabbage
50 g/2 oz/½ cup cheese, grated, to garnish soup

Place the joint, tied with string, in a flameproof casserole. Pour in the stock and season. Bring to the boil, skim, then lower the heat. Add the carrots, onions and bouquet garni. Cover and simmer for 1 hour.

Add the turnips, leeks and celery, both cut into 2.5-cm/1-inch lengths. Adjust seasoning and continue to simmer for an hour. Cut the cabbage into wedges, add to the pan and cook for 30 minutes longer.

Remove the joint and slice the meat. Arrange on a platter with the vegetables and serve with boiled potatoes, gherkins and a horseradish or tomato sauce.

Strain the stock, skim off any fat and serve as a soup. Pour the soup into individual bowls and garnish.

Serves 6–8

Rump steak with peppers and tomatoes

METRIC/IMPERIAL/AMERICAN
2 green peppers, halved lengthways and deseeded
2 onions, quartered
4 tablespoons/4 tablespoons/⅓ cup olive oil
4 tomatoes, peeled and cut into wedges
1 clove garlic, crushed
½ teaspoon dried oregano
salt and pepper
pinch cayenne pepper
25 g/1 oz/2 tablespoons butter
6 rump steaks
150 ml/¼ pint/⅔ cup red wine or beef stock

Grill the pepper halves under a hot grill to char and remove the skins. Slice.

Sauté the onions in half the oil. When softened add the peppers, tomatoes, garlic, oregano, salt, pepper and cayenne. Cook over a low heat for 10 minutes, stirring.

Meanwhile, heat the remaining oil and the butter in a large shallow flameproof casserole or gratin dish. Fry the steaks over a high heat for 1 minute only on each side. Drain off any excess fat. Add the sautéed vegetables and wine or stock. Bring to simmering point then place, uncovered, in the centre of a moderately hot oven (200°C, 400°F, Gas Mark 6) for 15–20 minutes.

Serves 6

Braised brisket

METRIC/IMPERIAL/AMERICAN
2 large onions, sliced
2 large carrots, sliced
2 cloves garlic
6–8 peppercorns
6 tablespoons/6 tablespoons/$\frac{1}{2}$ cup olive oil
bouquet garni
300 ml/$\frac{1}{2}$ pint/1$\frac{1}{4}$ cups red wine
1 tablespoon tomato purée
1.25–1.5 kg/2$\frac{1}{2}$–3 lb/2$\frac{1}{2}$–3 lb brisket
1 tablespoon chopped fresh herbs
1$\frac{1}{2}$ tablespoons/1$\frac{1}{2}$ tablespoons/2 tablespoons flour
450 ml/$\frac{3}{4}$ pint/2 cups beef stock

Place half the onion and carrot in a saucepan with 1 chopped clove garlic, peppercorns, a third of the olive oil, bouquet garni, wine and tomato purée. Bring to the boil and simmer for 2 minutes. Cool and pour over the meat. Marinate for 24 hours. Reserve the marinade. Push the herbs into the brisket. Rub the meat with garlic. Season. Heat the oil in a flameproof casserole and brown the meat. Remove. Sauté the remaining onion and carrot. Return the meat and pour the marinade over. Cover and cook in a moderate oven (160°C, 325°F, Gas Mark 3) for about 2–2$\frac{1}{2}$ hours. Mix the flour and stock. Bring to the boil and simmer for 15–20 minutes. Remove the meat. Strain juices and skim. Add to the stock and boil until thick. Carve the meat and pour the sauce over. Garnish with watercress.

Serves 6–8

Mediterranean pot roast

METRIC/IMPERIAL/AMERICAN
2 tablespoons/2 tablespoons/3 tablespoons olive oil
1.25 kg/2$\frac{1}{2}$ lb/2$\frac{1}{2}$ lb boned and rolled rib of beef
6 shallots
2 carrots, sliced
1 clove garlic, crushed
bouquet garni
salt and pepper
pinch nutmeg
200 ml/$\frac{1}{3}$ pint/$\frac{3}{4}$ cup red wine or beef stock
100 g/4 oz/$\frac{3}{4}$ cup green or black olives, stoned
BEURRE MANIÉ:
15 g/$\frac{1}{2}$ oz/1 tablespoon butter
15 g/$\frac{1}{2}$ oz/2 tablespoons flour

Heat the oil in a flameproof casserole and brown the meat on all sides over a low heat. Drain off excess fat.

Add the shallots, carrots, garlic, bouquet garni, salt, pepper and nutmeg. Pour the wine or stock over the meat and cover with a tight-fitting lid. Cook in a moderate oven (160°C, 325°F, Gas Mark 3) for 2 hours.

Add the olives to the casserole. Adjust seasoning. Return to the oven for a further 30 minutes or until tender.

Discard the bouquet garni. Slice the meat and keep warm. Blend the butter and flour together and add to the cooking liquid, a little at a time. Warm through to thicken. Pour over the meat.

Serves 6

Boeuf à la provençale

METRIC/IMPERIAL/AMERICAN
1 kg/2 lb/2 lb lean braising or stewing steak
3 tablespoons/3 tablespoons/¼ cup olive oil
175 g/6 oz/6 oz streaky bacon, chopped
225 g/8 oz/½ lb button onions
225 g/8 oz/1½ cups carrots, sliced
2 tablespoons/2 tablespoons/3 tablespoons tomato purée
3 cloves garlic, crushed
300 ml/½ pint/1¼ cups red wine
300 ml/½ pint/1¼ cups beef stock
bouquet garni
pinch dried thyme, salt and pepper
0.5 kg/1 lb/2 cups tomatoes, peeled and chopped
100 g/4 oz/¾ cup black olives, stoned
25 g/1 oz/2 tablespoons butter
25 g/1 oz/¼ cup flour
chopped parsley and triangles of fried bread to garnish

Cut the beef into 2.5-cm/1-inch squares. Heat the oil in a flameproof casserole and fry the beef until brown. Remove. Add the bacon, onions and carrot and sauté for 5 minutes. Stir in the tomato purée, garlic, wine, stock, bouquet garni, thyme and seasoning. Bring to the boil. Return the meat to the casserole, cover and cook in a cool oven (150°C, 300°F, Gas Mark 2) for 1½ hours. Add the tomatoes and olives and cook for 1 hour. Blend the butter into the flour. Add to the casserole a little at a time. Heat through but do not boil. Garnish.

Serves 4–6   *Illustrated on the cover*

Daube de boeuf

METRIC/IMPERIAL/AMERICAN
0.75–1 kg/1½–2 lb/1½–2 lb topside
flour for coating
3 tablespoons/3 tablespoons/¼ cup olive oil
50 g/2 oz/2 oz streaky bacon, chopped
225 g/8 oz/½ lb button onions
2 tomatoes, peeled and sliced
1 clove garlic, crushed
50 g/2 oz/⅓ cup raisins
25 g/1 oz/1 oz dried apricots, soaked and halved
1 teaspoon dried mixed herbs
2 bay leaves
300 ml/½ pint/1¼ cups red wine
150 ml/¼ pint/⅔ cup beef stock
salt and pepper

Cut the meat into 1-cm/½-inch slices and coat well with the flour. Heat the oil in a flameproof casserole and fry the meat until lightly browned all over. Remove and reserve. Sauté the bacon and onions in the fat in the pan for 3–4 minutes, then return the meat and add the remaining ingredients. Bring to simmering point then cover and place in a cool oven (150°C, 300°F, Gas Mark 2) for 2–2½ hours or until the meat is very tender. Discard the bay leaves. Serve with buttered new potatoes and a good red wine.

Serves 4–6

Beef with oranges

METRIC/IMPERIAL/AMERICAN
0.75–1 kg/1½–2 lb/1½–2 lb chuck steak
salt and pepper
3 tablespoons/3 tablespoons/¼ cup flour
3 tablespoons/3 tablespoons/¼ cup oil
2 onions, sliced
1 clove garlic, crushed
1 green pepper, deseeded and chopped
few drops Tabasco sauce
300 ml/½ pint/1¼ cups dry cider
300 ml/½ pint/1¼ cups beef stock
2 oranges
watercress sprig to garnish

Cut the meat into 2.5-cm/1-inch cubes and coat with seasoned
flour. Heat the oil in a flameproof casserole and fry the meat
quickly to seal. Remove from the casserole. Gently sauté the
onions, garlic and pepper then return the meat to the casserole.
Sprinkle in any remaining seasoned flour and cook, stirring, for
1 minute. Stir in the Tabasco sauce, cider and stock. Bring to
the boil, cover and cook in a moderate oven (160°C, 325°F, Gas
Mark 3) for 2 hours.
  Peel the oranges over a plate, removing all the pith. Cut the
flesh into segments and add to the casserole, together with any
juice that may have collected on the plate. Return to the oven
for a further 30 minutes. Garnish with watercress and serve
with plain boiled potatoes.

Serves 4–6

Tasty meatballs

METRIC/IMPERIAL/AMERICAN
MEATBALLS:
0.5 kg/1 lb/1 lb minced beef
225 g/8 oz/½ lb lean bacon, minced
1 onion, grated
1 clove garlic, crushed
1 teaspoon mixed dried herbs
1 egg, beaten
good pinch ground nutmeg
salt and pepper

2 tablespoons/2 tablespoons/3 tablespoons oil
2 carrots, thinly sliced
2 sticks celery, chopped
2 tablespoons/2 tablespoons/3 tablespoons flour
300 ml/½ pint/1¼ cups beef stock
1 (396-g/14-oz/14-oz) can tomatoes
2 teaspoons Worcestershire sauce

Mix together all the ingredients for the meatballs and shape the
mixture into 20 balls. Fry in the oil until browned. Remove and
keep warm. Add the carrots and celery to the pan and sauté.
  Arrange the meatballs and vegetables in a casserole. Add the
flour to the oil and stir in the stock, tomatoes and Worcestershire sauce. Bring to the boil, stirring. Season, then pour over
the meatballs. Cover and cook in a moderate oven (180°C,
350°F, Gas Mark 4) for 1 hour.

Serves 4–6

Carbonnade

METRIC/IMPERIAL/AMERICAN
1 kg/2 lb/2 lb braising steak
3 tablespoons/3 tablespoons/¼ cup cooking oil
100 g/4 oz/¼ lb streaky bacon, chopped
3 tablespoons/3 tablespoons/¼ cup flour
300 ml/½ pint/1¼ cups brown ale
300 ml/½ pint/1¼ cups beef stock
1 tablespoon wine vinegar
1 tablespoon soft brown sugar
salt and pepper
good pinch nutmeg
4 onions, sliced
2 cloves garlic, crushed
bouquet garni
2 bay leaves

Cut the meat into 2.5-cm/1-inch cubes and fry quickly in the oil. This may have to be done in several batches. Remove and keep warm. Fry the bacon in the remaining oil until golden. Keep warm with the meat.

Stir the flour into the pan and cook for 1 minute. Remove from the heat and add the beer, stock, vinegar, sugar, salt, pepper and nutmeg. Bring to the boil, stirring.

Place the meat and bacon in a casserole and add the onions, garlic, bouquet garni and bay leaves. Pour in the sauce, cover and cook in a cool oven (150°C, 300°F, Gas Mark 2) for 3 hours. Discard bouquet garni and bay leaves.

Serves 4

Beef olives

METRIC/IMPERIAL/AMERICAN
6 thin slices beef (sirloin, topside or rump)
225 g/8 oz/½ lb streaky bacon
2 cloves garlic, crushed
1 tablespoon chopped parsley
1 teaspoon chopped fresh thyme
salt and pepper
2 onions, finely chopped
1 carrot, grated
2 tablespoons/2 tablespoons/3 tablespoons oil
1 bay leaf
300 ml/½ pint/1¼ cups red wine and stock
15 g/½ oz/1 tablespoon butter
15 g/½ oz/2 tablespoons flour

Place the beef slices between sheets of greaseproof paper and beat until wafer-thin. Trim each slice to about 7 cm/3 inches wide and 10 cm/4 inches long. Mince the trimmings with the bacon and add garlic, parsley and thyme. Season. Divide between the beef slices and roll up. Tie each roll with fine string.

Sauté the onion and carrot in the oil. Place in a flameproof casserole. Brown the beef rolls in the pan. Drain and place on the vegetables. Add the bay leaf, wine and stock. Cover and cook in a moderate oven (160°C, 325°F, Gas Mark 3) for 1½ hours. Remove the string, keep the beef olives warm. Skim the sauce. Blend the butter into the flour and stir this into the sauce. Heat through. Pour the sauce over the beef olives.

Serves 6

Boeuf à la bourguignonne

METRIC/IMPERIAL/AMERICAN

1 kg/2 lb/2 lb chuck steak
3 tablespoons/3 tablespoons/¼ cup oil
175 g/6 oz/6 oz streaky bacon, diced
1–1½ tablespoons flour
450 ml/¾ pint/2 cups red wine
150 ml/¼ pint/⅔ cup beef stock
bouquet garni
2 cloves garlic, crushed
salt and pepper
20 button onions
25 g/1 oz/2 tablespoons butter
175 g/6 oz/1½ cups button mushrooms
parsley sprig to garnish

Cut the meat into 5-cm/2-inch squares. Heat the oil in a flameproof casserole and brown the meat. Remove the meat and keep warm. Add the bacon to the casserole and sauté until golden. Sprinkle in the flour. Cook for 1 minute, stirring, then remove from the heat and pour in the wine and stock. Add the bouquet garni and garlic and season. Bring to simmering point, stirring. Return the meat to the casserole, cover and place in a cool oven (150°C, 300°F, Gas Mark 2) for 2 hours.

Meanwhile, blanch the onions for 1 minute in boiling water, then sauté them gently in the butter. Add the onions and mushrooms to the casserole and cook for a further 30 minutes. Discard the bouquet garni. Garnish.

Serves 4–6

Hungarian goulash

METRIC/IMPERIAL/AMERICAN

0.75–1 kg/1½–2 lb/1½–2 lb skirt steak, cubed
3 tablespoons/3 tablespoons/¼ cup oil
3 onions, sliced
1 red pepper, deseeded and chopped
25 g/1 oz/¼ cup flour
2 tablespoons/2 tablespoons/3 tablespoons paprika pepper
0.5 kg/1 lb/2 cups tomatoes, peeled and chopped
600 ml/1 pint/2½ cups beef stock
bouquet garni
1 teaspoon dried thyme
salt
150 ml/¼ pint/⅔ cup soured cream
parsley sprig to garnish

Sauté the meat in the oil in a flameproof casserole; remove.

Lower the heat and sauté the onions and red pepper in the fat remaining in the casserole. When they are softened sprinkle in the flour and paprika pepper. Cook, stirring, for 1 minute. Add the tomatoes and stock and bring to simmering point, stirring continuously. Return the meat to the casserole and add the bouquet garni and thyme. Season with salt to taste. Cover and place in a moderate oven (160°C, 325°F, Gas Mark 3) for 2½–3 hours. Remove the bouquet garni. Spoon a little of the soured cream on top of the goulash to garnish with the parsley, and serve the remainder separately.

Serves 4

Dijon beef

METRIC/IMPERIAL/AMERICAN
1.25 kg/2½ lb/2½ lb topside
3 tablespoons/3 tablespoons/¼ cup Dijon mustard
2 tablespoons/2 tablespoons/3 tablespoons flour
5 tablespoons/5 tablespoons/6 tablespoons olive oil
0.5 kg/1 lb/1 lb onions, sliced
salt and pepper
1 bay leaf
1 teaspoon chopped fresh thyme
450 ml/¾ pint/2 cups beef stock or stock and red wine
chopped parsley to garnish

Cut the beef into 5-mm/¼-inch slices, removing any fat. Spread both sides of the slices liberally with mustard, cover and keep in the refrigerator overnight. Coat in flour and brown the slices lightly in the olive oil. This will probably have to be done in 2 or 3 batches. Arrange alternate layers of meat and onion in a casserole, lightly seasoning each meat layer and finishing with a layer of onion. Add the bay leaf, thyme and stock. Cover and cook in a moderate oven (160°C, 325°F, Gas Mark 3) for 2–2½ hours. Discard the bay leaf. Garnish with chopped parsley.

Serves 6

Beef hotpot with herb dumplings

METRIC/IMPERIAL/AMERICAN
0.75–1 kg/1½–2 lb/1½–2 lb braising steak, cubed
seasoned flour
3 tablespoons/3 tablespoons/¼ cup oil
2 onions, sliced
4 leeks, trimmed and sliced
6 carrots, sliced
1 (396-g/14-oz/14-oz) can tomatoes
450 ml/¾ pint/2 cups stock or red wine
100 g/4 oz/1 cup self-raising flour
50 g/2 oz/½ cup shredded suet
2 teaspoons chopped fresh thyme or 1 teaspoon dried
2 teaspoons chopped fresh sage or 1 teaspoon dried
100 g/4 oz/1 cup mushrooms, sliced

Coat the meat with seasoned flour. Heat the oil in a flameproof casserole and fry the meat quickly to seal. Remove. Fry the onions, leeks and carrots until softened. Add the tomatoes and stock or wine. Bring to the boil, stirring, then return the meat. Season. Cover and cook in a moderate oven (160°C, 325°F, Gas Mark 3) for 2 hours.

Mix the flour and suet, add the herbs and season. Stir in cold water to make an elastic dough and divide into 12 portions. After 2 hours, stir in mushrooms. Place the dumplings around the edge and return to the oven for 15–20 minutes.

Serves 6

Lamb casseroles

The important point to remember about lamb casseroles is that the main cuts which are used – breast, middle, neck and scrag – are fatty and do need to be trimmed of as much fat as possible before cooking. Chump chops and cutlets may be casseroled as a change from grilling and minced lamb is ideal for such favourites as moussaka; a stuffed shoulder of lamb is delicious when braised or pot-roasted.

Lamb chops paprika

METRIC/IMPERIAL/AMERICAN
8 loin or chump chops
salt and pepper
2 tablespoons/2 tablespoons/3 tablespoons flour
25 g/1 oz/2 tablespoons butter
1 onion, chopped
1 green pepper, deseeded and chopped
2 tablespoons/2 tablespoons/3 tablespoons paprika
 pepper
pinch cayenne pepper
1 (396-g/14-oz/14-oz) can tomatoes

Trim any excess fat from the chops and coat in seasoned flour. Heat the butter in a flameproof casserole and brown the chops on both sides. Remove from the casserole. Add the onion and green pepper and continue to sauté until softened. Sprinkle in the paprika pepper and cayenne and cook for 1 minute. Place the chops back in the casserole. Pour in the tomatoes with their juice and adjust seasoning, if necessary. Cover and cook in a moderate oven (160°C, 325°F, Gas Mark 3) for 1–1½ hours. Skim well before serving. Serve with peas.

Serves 4

Breast of lamb with mixed herbs

METRIC/IMPERIAL/AMERICAN
1 kg/2 lb/2 lb boned breast of lamb
salt and pepper
2 tablespoons/2 tablespoons/3 tablespoons flour
25 g/1 oz/2 tablespoons butter
25 g/1 oz/¼ cup flour
1 onion, chopped
1 tablespoon chopped parsley
1 tablespoon chopped fresh sage
1 tablespoon chopped fresh thyme
600 ml/1 pint/2½ cups chicken stock
juice of ½ lemon
2 tablespoons/2 tablespoons/3 tablespoons cream

Remove the skin from the meat and cut into 4-cm/1½-inch pieces and coat in seasoned flour. Sauté gently in the butter. Place the meat in a casserole. Sauté the onion until softened but not coloured. Stir in the flour and cook for 1 minute, then add to the meat. Add the chopped herbs.

Sprinkle any remaining seasoned flour into the pan to soak up the fat, cook for 1 minute then stir in the stock. Bring to the boil and pour over the meat. Cover and cook in a moderately hot oven (180°C, 350°F, Gas Mark 4) for 1–1½ hours. Skim and stir in the lemon juice and cream. Sprinkle with more chopped herbs.

Serves 4–6

Mixed meats cassoulet

METRIC/IMPERIAL/AMERICAN
4 tablespoons/4 tablespoons/⅓ cup olive oil
2 tablespoons/2 tablespoons/3 tablespoons lemon juice
2 cloves garlic, crushed
salt and freshly ground black pepper
0.5 kg/1 lb/1 lb boned lamb shoulder, cubed
225 g/8 oz/½ lb lean pork, cubed
225 g/8 oz/½ lb rump steak, cubed
3 onions, sliced
450 ml/¾ pint/2 cups dry white wine
1 teaspoon chopped fresh sage
1 teaspoon chopped fresh thyme
1 bay leaf
0.75 kg/1½ lb/1½ lb potatoes, peeled and diced
15 g/½ oz/2 tablespoons cornflour
chopped parsley to garnish

Mix together the olive oil, lemon juice and garlic. Season and pour over the meats; marinate overnight in the refrigerator.

Place the meats and marinade in a flameproof casserole, top with the onion and pour in the wine. Add the herbs and bring to simmering point. Cover and place in a moderate oven (180°C, 350°F, Gas Mark 4) for 45 minutes. Cook the potatoes for 5 minutes in boiling salted water, drain. Skim the casserole and remove the bay leaf. Mix the cornflour with a little water, then stir into the casserole. Mix in the potatoes, cover and return to the oven for a further 20 minutes. Garnish.

Serves 4–6

Moussaka

METRIC/IMPERIAL/AMERICAN
2–3 aubergines, sliced
salt and pepper
olive oil for shallow frying
4–5 onions, sliced
0.5 kg/1 lb/1 lb lamb, minced
1 (140-g/5-oz/5-oz) can tomato purée
150 ml/¼ pint/⅔ cup stock
½ teaspoon garlic salt
2 eggs
150 ml/¼ pint/⅔ cup natural yogurt, single cream or
   creamy milk
parsley sprig to garnish

Sprinkle the aubergines with salt and leave for 30 minutes.
Rinse the slices and dry. Fry in oil until golden, then drain on
absorbent paper. Sauté the onions in oil for 5 minutes. Fry the
lamb in a dry pan to lightly brown, then drain.
   Line the bottom of an ovenproof dish with half the aubergine
slices. Cover with a layer of half the onions, then half the lamb.
Season and repeat.
   Mix the tomato purée with the stock and the garlic salt.
Spread this sauce over the top layer of lamb and place in a
moderate oven (180°C, 350°F, Gas Mark 4) for 30 minutes. Beat
together the eggs and yogurt, season well and pour over the
moussaka. Return to the oven for about 15–20 minutes.
Garnish.

Serves 4

Lamb with lentils

METRIC/IMPERIAL/AMERICAN
175 g/6 oz/¾ cup lentils
1 kg/2 lb/2 lb boned shoulder of lamb
2 tablespoons/2 tablespoons/3 tablespoons oil
2 carrots, sliced
2 onions, chopped
1–2 cloves garlic, crushed
2 bay leaves
bouquet garni
good pinch nutmeg
salt and pepper
450 ml/¾ pint/2 cups chicken or beef stock
chopped parsley to garnish

Soak the lentils in cold water for 2 hours.
   Meanwhile, cut the meat into 4-cm/1½-inch pieces, removing
any excess fat. Heat the oil in a flameproof casserole and brown
the meat on all sides over moderate heat. Remove from the
casserole. Sauté the carrots and onions until softened then
return the meat to the casserole. Add the garlic, bay leaves,
bouquet garni, nutmeg and seasoning. Pour over the stock,
bring to the boil, cover and place in a moderate oven (180°C,
350°F, Gas Mark 4) for 30 minutes.
   Drain the lentils, add to the casserole and return to the oven
for a further 45 minutes. Remove the bay leaves and bouquet
garni. Serve garnished with chopped parsley.

Serves 4–6

Navarin of lamb

METRIC/IMPERIAL/AMERICAN
25 g/1 oz/2 tablespoons dripping or butter
1 kg/2 lb/2 lb best end of neck lamb cutlets
225 g/8 oz/½ lb young carrots
225 g/8 oz/½ lb button onions
2 young turnips, quartered
1 tablespoon sugar
1 tablespoon flour
600 ml/1 pint/2½ cups stock
salt and pepper
bouquet garni
8 small new potatoes
chopped parsley to garnish

Heat the dripping or butter in a flameproof casserole and brown the cutlets on both sides. Remove from the casserole. Add the carrots, onions and turnips to the casserole and sprinkle with the sugar. Sauté gently until browned, then stir in the flour. Cook for 1 minute. Gradually add the stock and season well. Bring to the boil, stirring continuously. Return the meat to the casserole, add the bouquet garni, cover and place in a moderate oven (160°C, 325°F, Gas Mark 3) for 45 minutes.

Scrape the potatoes and add to the casserole. Return to the oven for a further 45 minutes. Discard the bouquet garni and garnish with parsley. Serve with crusty French bread, if liked.

Serves 4

Lamb in yogurt and mint sauce

METRIC/IMPERIAL/AMERICAN
3 tablespoons/3 tablespoons/¼ cup oil
0.75–1 kg/1½–2 lb/1½–2 lb lean lamb, cubed
2 onions, sliced
1 tablespoon flour
300 ml/½ pint/1¼ cups white wine
bouquet garni
2 cloves garlic, crushed
salt and pepper
pinch nutmeg
2 tablespoons/2 tablespoons/3 tablespoons chopped mint
150 ml/¼ pint/⅔ cup natural yogurt
mint sprig to garnish

Heat the oil in a flameproof casserole and brown the meat. Remove the lamb and gently sauté the onions until softened. Sprinkle in the flour. Cook, stirring, for 1 minute, then pour in the wine. Bring to the boil, stirring continuously, then lower the heat. Replace the meat, add the bouquet garni, garlic, salt, pepper and nutmeg. Cover and place in a moderate oven (160°C, 325°F, Gas Mark 3) for 1–1½ hours or until the meat is tender.

Mix the chopped mint into the yogurt and stir the yogurt into the casserole. Reheat gently but do not boil. Garnish and serve with boiled rice.

Serves 4

Lamb fillet in cream sauce

METRIC/IMPERIAL/AMERICAN
1 kg/2 lb/2 lb lamb fillet
50 g/2 oz/$\frac{1}{4}$ cup butter
4 shallots, chopped
1 tablespoon flour
450 ml/$\frac{3}{4}$ pint/2 cups chicken stock
2 tablespoons/2 tablespoons/3 tablespoons lemon juice
225 g/8 oz/$\frac{1}{2}$ lb button mushrooms
1 rosemary sprig, divided, or $\frac{1}{2}$ teaspoon dried
salt and pepper
2 egg yolks
150 ml/$\frac{1}{4}$ pint/$\frac{2}{3}$ cup single cream

Cut the lamb into 2.5-cm/1-inch pieces. Melt the butter in a
flameproof casserole and sauté the lamb with the shallots. Do
not allow the meat to brown. Sauté until the shallots are
softened but not coloured. Sprinkle the flour into the casserole
and cook for 1 minute. Stir in the stock and the lemon juice.
Add the mushrooms, rosemary and seasoning. Bring to the
boil, stirring continuously, cover and cook in a moderate oven
(160°C, 325°F, Gas Mark 3) for 1 hour or until the meat is
tender.

Beat together the egg yolks and cream and stir in
2 tablespoons/2 tablespoons/3 tablespoons of the sauce from
the casserole. Blend the mixture into the casserole and warm
through over gentle heat until thickened. Do not allow to boil.
Adjust seasoning if necessary.

Serves 4

Irish stew

METRIC/IMPERIAL/AMERICAN
1 kg/2 lb/2 lb middle neck lamb chops
salt and freshly ground black pepper
225 g/8 oz/$\frac{1}{2}$ lb onions, sliced
4 carrots, sliced
2 sticks celery, chopped
2 teaspoons dried mixed herbs
0.5 kg/1 lb/1 lb potatoes, diced
300–450 ml/$\frac{1}{2}$–$\frac{3}{4}$ pint/1$\frac{1}{4}$–2 cups light stock
25 g/1 oz/2 tablespoons butter

Place the chops in a casserole, season and cover with the
vegetables. Sprinkle with half the herbs and top with the diced
potato. Season and pour over the stock so that it just comes up
to the layer of potato. Cover and place in a moderate oven
(180°C, 350°F, Gas Mark 4) for 2 hours.

Uncover the casserole, sprinkle the potatoes with the
remaining herbs and dot with the butter. Raise the oven
temperature to 200°C, 400°F, Gas Mark 6 and return the
casserole to the oven for 30 minutes to brown.

Serves 4–6

Braised stuffed shoulder of lamb

METRIC/IMPERIAL/AMERICAN
STUFFING:
50 g/2 oz/1 cup fresh breadcrumbs
2 rashers streaky bacon, finely chopped
1 onion, finely chopped
1 clove garlic, crushed
1 tablespoon chopped fresh mint, tarragon and parsley or
    1 teaspoon each dried
grated rind and juice of $\frac{1}{2}$ lemon
salt and pepper
1 egg, beaten

1 (1.5-kg/3$\frac{1}{2}$-lb/3$\frac{1}{2}$-lb) shoulder of lamb, boned
2 tablespoons/2 tablespoons/3 tablespoons oil
8 small whole carrots
4 sticks celery, chopped
300 ml/$\frac{1}{2}$ pint/1$\frac{1}{4}$ cups stock

Mix together all the stuffing ingredients and spread over the
boned side of the lamb. Roll up and tie with string. Brown the
meat in the oil, drain and place in a flameproof casserole. Sauté
carrots and celery and add to meat with stock. Cover and cook
in a moderate oven (180°C, 350°F, Gas Mark 4) for 2 hours.
Remove meat and vegetables. Thicken the sauce if liked. Slice
the meat, add the vegetables and pour the sauce over.

Serves 6–8

Leg of lamb with macedoine of vegetables

METRIC/IMPERIAL/AMERICAN
1 (1.5-kg/3$\frac{1}{2}$-lb/3$\frac{1}{2}$-lb) leg of lamb
2 tablespoons/2 tablespoons/3 tablespoons oil
2 onions
4 carrots, diced
2 leeks, sliced
2 tablespoons/2 tablespoons/3 tablespoons tomato purée
1 (396-g/14-oz/14-oz) can tomatoes
1 clove garlic, crushed
bouquet garni
salt and pepper

Brown the meat on all sides in the oil. Drain well and place in a
large casserole. Arrange the onions, carrots and leeks around
the meat and pour over the tomato purée mixed with the
tomatoes and their juice. Add the garlic, bouquet garni and
seasoning. Cover and cook in a moderate oven (180°C, 350°F,
Gas Mark 4) for 1$\frac{1}{4}$–1$\frac{1}{2}$ hours. Discard the bouquet garni and
serve the lamb surrounded by the vegetables.

Serves 6–8

Shoulder of lamb boulangère

METRIC/IMPERIAL/AMERICAN

1 (1.5-kg/3½-lb/3½-lb) shoulder of lamb, boned and rolled
2 cloves garlic, sliced
0.75 kg/1½ lb/1½ lb potatoes, sliced
1 teaspoon fresh chopped thyme or ½ teaspoon dried thyme
1 large fresh rosemary sprig, chopped, or ½ teaspoon dried rosemary
salt and pepper
75 g/3 oz/6 tablespoons butter
watercress to garnish

Make several small cuts in the skin of the lamb and insert the garlic slices. Arrange a layer of potato slices in the bottom of a large lightly greased casserole. Sprinkle with half the herbs and place the lamb on top. Arrange the remaining potato slices around the lamb and sprinkle with the rest of the herbs. Season and dot with the butter. Cover with a lid or foil and place in a moderately hot oven (180°C, 350°F, Gas Mark 4) for 1 hour. Uncover and increase the oven temperature to 200°C, 400°F, Gas Mark 6 for 15–30 minutes to brown the meat and potatoes. Garnish with watercress.

Serves 6

Lamb stew with prunes and apricots

METRIC/IMPERIAL/AMERICAN

1.75 kg/2½ lb/2½ lb middle neck lamb chops
25 g/1 oz/2 tablespoons butter
2 onions, sliced
1½ tablespoons/1½ tablespoons/2 tablespoons flour
300 ml/½ pint/1¼ cups chicken stock
300 ml/½ pint/1¼ cups red wine
bouquet garni
1 clove garlic, crushed
100 g/4 oz/⅔ cup prunes, soaked overnight
50 g/2 oz/⅓ cup dried apricots, soaked overnight
salt and pepper
1 teaspoon soft brown sugar

Brown the meat in the butter in a flameproof casserole. Remove and add the onions to the casserole and sauté until softened. Sprinkle in the flour and cook, stirring, over a low heat until the flour begins to brown. Gradually blend in the stock and wine and add the bouquet garni and garlic. Bring to the boil, stirring continuously, then reduce the heat, return the meat to the casserole and add the drained prunes and apricots. Season with salt, pepper and sugar. Cover and place in a moderate oven (180°C, 350°F, Gas Mark 4) for 1½ hours. Skim well before serving.

Serves 6

Lamb curry

METRIC/IMPERIAL/AMERICAN
1 kg/2 lb/2 lb lean shoulder of lamb
50 g/2 oz/¼ cup ghee or butter
2 onions, sliced
2 cloves garlic, crushed
25 g/1 oz/¼ cup flour
1-cm/½-inch/½-inch piece root ginger, finely chopped
1 teaspoon ground coriander
1½ teaspoons garam masala
300 ml/½ pint/1¼ cups chicken stock
salt and pepper
pinch chilli powder
150 ml/¼ pint/⅔ cup natural yogurt
flaked almonds and chopped parsley to garnish

Cut the meat into 2.5-cm/1-inch pieces. Heat the ghee or butter
in a saucepan or flameproof casserole and sauté the lamb until
evenly brown. Remove the meat and reserve. Sauté the onions
and garlic in the remaining fat until softened, then sprinkle in
the flour and cook for 1 minute. Return the meat to the pan and
sprinkle in the ginger, coriander and garam masala. Mix well
and cook for 2 minutes before pouring in the stock. Bring to the
boil and season to taste with salt, pepper and chilli powder.
Cover and simmer on top of the cooker or in a moderate oven
(160°C, 325°F, Gas Mark 3) for 1–1½ hours until the meat is
tender and the flavours have blended. Stir in the yogurt and heat
through but do not allow to boil. Garnish.

Serves 4–6

Lancashire hotpot

METRIC/IMPERIAL/AMERICAN
1 kg/2 lb/2 lb middle neck lamb chops
1 kg/2 lb/2 lb potatoes
0.5 kg/1 lb/1 lb onions
salt and pepper
300–450 ml/½–¾ pint/1¼–2 cups light stock

Trim any excess fat from the lamb. Peel and slice the potatoes
and onions. Place a layer of half the onions in the bottom of a
saucepan or flameproof casserole, then half the chops and half
the potatoes, seasoning each layer. Repeat. Pour over almost
enough stock to cover. Bring to the boil, cover and simmer on
the top of the cooker or place in a moderate oven (180°C, 350°F,
Gas Mark 4) for 2½ hours.

Serves 4–6

Pork casseroles

Any lean boneless piece of pork is suitable for casseroles – it may be cut from the belly, shoulder, leg or fillet – chump or loin chops or spare rib cutlets may also be casseroled. Many herbs go naturally with pork – try rosemary, sage, thyme, basil or marjoram. Use dry cider as some or all of the cooking liquid in pork casseroles as it makes a delicious change. Included in this section are recipes using bacon joints.

Pork fillet au porto

METRIC/IMPERIAL/AMERICAN
0.75 kg/1½ lb/1½ lb pork fillet
salt and pepper
25 g/1 oz/¼ cup flour
25 g/1 oz/2 tablespoons butter
2 onions, chopped
1 tablespoon Worcestershire sauce
1 tablespoon mushroom ketchup
2 tablespoons/2 tablespoons/3 tablespoons redcurrant
   jelly
2 tablespoons/2 tablespoons/3 tablespoons tomato purée
4 tablespoons/4 tablespoons/⅓ cup port
4 tablespoons/4 tablespoons/⅓ cup double cream
chopped parsley to garnish

Remove the outer skin from the pork fillet and cut into 2.5-cm/1-inch slices. Coat with seasoned flour and sauté in the butter until golden. Transfer the meat to a casserole. Sauté the onions until softened in the butter remaining in the pan then transfer to the casserole with the meat. Mix together the remaining ingredients, except the cream, and pour over the pork and onions. Cover and cook in a moderate oven (180°C, 350°F, Gas Mark 4) for 30–40 minutes or until the meat is tender. Spoon the cream over the meat and return, uncovered, to the oven for 5 minutes to heat through. Sprinkle with chopped parsley.

Serves 4

Pork and beans

METRIC/IMPERIAL/AMERICAN
225 g/8 oz/1 cup haricot or butter beans
salt
3 tablespoons/3 tablespoons/¼ cup olive oil
1 kg/2 lb/2 lb lean pork, cubed
25 g/1 oz/¼ cup flour
pepper
0.5 kg/1 lb/1 lb onions, sliced
2–3 cloves garlic, sliced
600 ml/1 pint/2½ cups beef stock
4 tablespoons/4 tablespoons/⅓ cup tomato purée
1 tablespoon Worcestershire sauce

Soak the beans in cold water overnight. Drain and place in a large saucepan with enough fresh cold water to cover. Add a little salt and bring to the boil. Simmer for 1 hour.

Meanwhile, heat the oil in a large flameproof casserole. Coat the meat in seasoned flour and brown on all sides over a moderate heat. Drain off any excess fat and arrange the onions and garlic on top of the meat. Pour in the stock with the tomato purée and Worcestershire sauce. Bring to the boil, cover and place in a moderate oven (160°C, 325°F, Gas Mark 3) for 1 hour.

Drain the haricot or butter beans and add to the casserole. Adjust seasoning if necessary. Re-cover and return to the oven for a further hour or until the meat is tender and the beans are cooked.

Serves 6

Pork ragoût

METRIC/IMPERIAL/AMERICAN
1 kg/2 lb/2 lb boned belly of pork
2 onions, sliced
225 g/8 oz/½ lb baby carrots
1 bay leaf
2 teaspoons chopped fresh sage or 1 teaspoon dried sage
1 tablespoon flour
150 ml/¼ pint/⅔ cup chicken stock
1 (396-g/14-oz/14-oz) can tomatoes
salt and pepper
0.5 kg/1 lb/1 lb fresh peas, shelled
6 medium potatoes, peeled and quartered
1 teaspoon sugar

Cut the meat into strips, removing excess fat. Fry in a dry pan until brown. Drain and place in a large casserole. Sauté the onions in the pork fat until soft, then add to the casserole, together with the carrots and herbs. Sprinkle the flour into the fat remaining in the pan and cook for 1 minute, stirring. Gradually blend in the stock and tomatoes and bring to the boil, stirring. Season to taste, then pour over the meat and vegetables. Cover and place in a moderate oven (160°C, 325°F, Gas Mark 3) for 1¼ hours.

Add the peas, potatoes and sugar. Re-cover and return to the oven for a further 45 minutes or until the peas and potatoes are tender. Remove the bay leaf before serving.

Serves 6

Normandy pork

METRIC/IMPERIAL/AMERICAN
1 kg/2 lb/2 lb boned shoulder of pork, cubed
3 tablespoons/3 tablespoons/¼ cup oil
2 large onions, sliced
1 clove garlic, crushed
3 tablespoons/3 tablespoons/¼ cup flour
300 ml/½ pint/1¼ cups chicken stock
300 ml/½ pint/1¼ cups dry cider
½ teaspoon dried basil
½ teaspoon dried marjoram
salt and pepper
2 eating apples
3 tablespoons/3 tablespoons/¼ cup double cream
chopped parsley to garnish

Heat the oil in a flameproof casserole and sauté the pork over a moderate heat until golden. Remove the meat and add the onions and garlic to the casserole. Sauté gently until beginning to colour. Sprinkle in the flour, mix well and cook for 1 minute. Gradually blend in the stock and cider and bring to the boil, stirring constantly. Return the pork to the casserole, add the herbs and season to taste. Cover and place in a moderate oven (180°C, 350°F, Gas Mark 4) for 45 minutes. Peel, core and slice the apples, reserving some slices for garnish, and add to the casserole. Return to the oven for a further 45 minutes or until the meat is tender. Stir the cream into the casserole before serving. Garnish with parsley and reserved slices of apple.

Serves 4–6

Pork chops with ham

METRIC/IMPERIAL/AMERICAN
25 g/1 oz/2 tablespoons butter
4 lean pork loin chops
4 shallots, finely chopped
1 (225-g/8-oz/½-lb) piece ham or gammon, diced
300 ml/½ pint/1¼ cups dry white wine or wine and
    chicken stock
bouquet garni
salt and pepper
1 tablespoon cornflour
watercress to garnish

Heat the butter in a flameproof casserole and brown the chops gently on both sides. Add the shallots to soften, then add the diced ham. Pour in the wine, add the bouquet garni and season to taste. Cover and place in a moderate oven (180°C, 350°F, Gas Mark 4) for 1 hour or until tender.

Remove the meat and keep warm. Discard the bouquet garni. Mix the cornflour with a little water and stir in 2 tablespoons/2 tablespoons/3 tablespoons of the sauce from the casserole. Blend this mixture into the casserole, off the heat. Cook the sauce over a low heat, stirring continuously, until it is smooth and has thickened slightly. Adjust the seasoning if necessary and pour the sauce over the chops and ham on a warmed platter or return the meat to the casserole. Garnish with watercress and serve with ratatouille, if liked.

Serves 4

Pork with lemon

METRIC/IMPERIAL/AMERICAN
0.75–1 kg/1½–2 lb/1½–2 lb pork fillet, sliced
salt and pepper
3 tablespoons/3 tablespoons/¼ cup flour
2 onions, sliced
50 g/2 oz/¼ cup butter
1 tablespoon oil
1 (396-g/14-oz/14-oz) can tomatoes
150 ml/¼ pint/⅔ cup chicken stock
2 lemons
1 teaspoon chopped fresh thyme or ½ teaspoon dried
   thyme
1 teaspoon chopped fresh tarragon or ½ teaspoon dried
   tarragon
watercress to garnish

Coat the pork with seasoned flour and sauté with the onions in the butter and oil in a flameproof casserole. When the meat has lightly browned, add the tomatoes with their juice, stock and the juice and grated rind of 1 lemon. Sprinkle in the herbs and adjust the seasoning if necessary. Cover and place in a moderate oven (160°C, 325°F, Gas Mark 3) for 1 hour. Garnish with the remaining lemon cut into wedges and watercress. Serve with rice or noodles.

Serves 4

Indian pork

METRIC/IMPERIAL/AMERICAN
1 kg/2 lb/2 lb lean pork
½ teaspoon cumin seeds
2 cloves garlic
5 peppercorns
½ teaspoon ground turmeric
½ teaspoon ground coriander
6 tablespoons/6 tablespoons/½ cup wine vinegar
2 tablespoons/2 tablespoons/3 tablespoons oil
1 (2.5-cm/1-inch/1-inch) piece root ginger, finely
   chopped
2 fresh chillis, finely chopped
1 onion, chopped
300 ml/½ pint/1¼ cups beef stock
salt and pepper

Cut the pork into cubes. Grind the cumin seeds, garlic and peppercorns in a wooden or plastic bowl, and mix with the turmeric, coriander and vinegar. Coat the pork pieces with this mixture, cover and allow to marinate overnight.

   Heat the oil in a flameproof casserole and sauté the ginger, chillis and onion for 5 minutes. Drain off any excess fat and add the pork with the marinade. Pour in the stock, season to taste and bring to the boil. Reduce the heat, cover and simmer gently for 1½ hours or until the pork is tender. Serve with boiled rice.

Serves 4–6

Braised gammon

METRIC/IMPERIAL/AMERICAN
1 (1.25-kg/2½-lb/2½-lb) piece gammon or bacon
6–8 carrots
2 bay leaves
6 cloves
3 onions, finely sliced
2 sticks celery, finely chopped
150 ml/¼ pint/⅔ cup white wine or chicken stock
freshly ground black pepper

Soak the gammon or bacon in cold water overnight. Drain, place in a large saucepan and cover with fresh cold water. Add the carrots, bay leaves and cloves. Bring to the boil slowly, skim well, cover and simmer gently for 35 minutes.

Drain again and place the gammon and carrots in a large casserole. Add the onions and celery. Pour in the wine or stock and season to taste with freshly ground black pepper. Cover and place in a moderate oven (180°C, 350°F, Gas Mark 4) for 35–45 minutes. Serve with courgettes and parsley sauce to which the cooking juices can be added, if liked.

Serves 6–8

Sweet and sour bacon

METRIC/IMPERIAL/AMERICAN
1 (0.75–1-kg/1½–2-lb/1½–2-lb) bacon joint
4 tomatoes, peeled, deseeded and chopped
1 green pepper, deseeded and chopped
1 onion, sliced
1 (425-g/15-oz/15-oz) can pineapple tidbits
1 tablespoon cornflour
2 tablespoons/2 tablespoons/3 tablespoons soy sauce
1 tablespoon soft brown sugar
2 tablespoons/2 tablespoons/3 tablespoons wine vinegar
1 tablespoon clear honey
salt and pepper

Soak the bacon joint in cold water for 6 hours or overnight. Drain well, then cut into 1-cm/½-inch cubes.

Place in a casserole with the tomatoes, pepper and onion. Drain the pineapple, reserving the juice, and add the fruit to the casserole.

Blend a little pineapple juice with the cornflour, then place the remaining pineapple juice, soy sauce, soft brown sugar, vinegar and honey in a small saucepan and bring to boiling point. Then pour on to the blended cornflour. Return to the saucepan and allow to thicken. Pour the sauce over the ingredients in the casserole. Cover and cook in a moderate oven (180°C, 350°F, Gas Mark 4) for 1½ hours. Serve with plain boiled rice, if liked.

Serves 4–6

Veal casseroles

This delicately flavoured meat needs careful cooking to do it justice and is therefore ideal for casseroles. Boned and stuffed shoulder or breast and middle neck of veal may be pot-roasted or braised; boneless pie veal, usually cut from the neck or knuckle, and thick cutlets from the best end of neck are also suitable. Use judicious amounts of seasonings and herbs in veal dishes to avoid masking the delicate flavour of the meat.

Veal and orange casserole

METRIC/IMPERIAL/AMERICAN
1 kg/2 lb/2 lb stewing veal, trimmed and cubed
salt and pepper
flour for coating
25 g/1 oz/2 tablespoons butter
1 tablespoon oil
2 onions, sliced
3 carrots, sliced (optional)
2 cloves garlic, crushed
300 ml/$\frac{1}{2}$ pint/$1\frac{1}{4}$ cups chicken stock
juice of 4 oranges
1 teaspoon lemon juice
1–2 teaspoons arrowroot (optional)
GARNISH:
1 tablespoon grated orange rind
chopped parsley

Coat the meat in seasoned flour. Heat the butter and oil in a flameproof casserole and gently sauté the veal, onions, carrots, if used, and garlic for 5 minutes. Drain off any excess fat and pour in the stock mixed with the orange and lemon juice. Bring to the boil, cover and cook in a moderate oven (180°C, 350°F, Gas Mark 4) for $1\frac{1}{2}$ hours.

If liked, the liquid can be thickened with the arrowroot mixed to a paste with a little water. Add the blended arrowroot to the casserole and stir over gentle heat until the sauce thickens. Garnish with grated orange rind and chopped parsley.

Serves 4–6

Veal with courgettes

METRIC/IMPERIAL/AMERICAN
3 tablespoons/3 tablespoons/¼ cup oil
1 kg/2 lb/2 lb stewing veal, cubed
2 onions, chopped
1 clove garlic, crushed
1 green pepper, deseeded and chopped
300 ml/½ pint/1¼ cups dry white wine
300 ml/½ pint/1¼ cups chicken stock
bouquet garni
½ teaspoon dried mixed herbs
salt and pepper
0.5 kg/1 lb/1 lb courgettes
25 g/1 oz/2 tablespoons butter
25 g/1 oz/¼ cup flour
chopped parsley and triangles of fried bread to garnish

Heat the oil in a flameproof casserole and gently sauté the meat until golden. Add the onions, garlic and green pepper, and continue to sauté until the vegetables are softened. Drain off any excess oil and pour in the wine and stock. Add the bouquet garni and herbs and season. Bring to the boil, cover and place in a moderate oven (180°C, 350°F, Gas Mark 4) for 1 hour.

Slice the courgettes and add to the casserole. Mix well and return to the oven for a further 30 minutes. Remove the bouquet garni. Blend together the butter and flour and stir into the casserole, a little at a time. Heat through until thickened. Garnish.

Serves 4–6

Cheesy veal chops

METRIC/IMPERIAL/AMERICAN
25 g/1 oz/2 tablespoons butter
6 veal chops
3 onions, finely chopped
2 sticks celery, finely chopped
2 cloves garlic, crushed
1 (396-g/14-oz/14-oz) can tomatoes
1 teaspoon dried oregano
4 tablespoons/4 tablespoons/⅓ cup tomato purée
salt and freshly ground black pepper
75 g/3 oz/¾ cup Cheddar cheese, grated

Heat the butter in a saucepan or large frying pan and brown the chops on both sides. Remove and keep warm. Add the onions, celery and garlic to the fat remaining in the pan and sauté gently for 5 minutes until soft but not coloured. Add the tomatoes with their juice, oregano, tomato purée and seasoning. Simmer, covered, for 5 minutes. Place the chops in the bottom of a shallow casserole and pour the tomato sauce over. Cover and cook in a moderate oven (180°C, 350°F, Gas Mark 4) for 45 minutes or until tender. Sprinkle with the grated cheese and either place in a hot oven (220°C, 425°F, Gas Mark 7) or under a preheated grill until golden and bubbling. Serve immediately.

Serves 6

Veal méditerranée

METRIC/IMPERIAL/AMERICAN
1 large aubergine
salt
5 tablespoons/5 tablespoons/6 tablespoons olive oil
1 kg/2 lb/2 lb shoulder of veal, cubed
8 small whole onions
1 green pepper, deseeded and chopped
1 red pepper, deseeded and chopped
0.5 kg/1 lb/1 lb tomatoes, peeled and chopped
2 teaspoons chopped fresh marjoram or 1 teaspoon dried
  marjoram
300 ml/½ pint/1¼ cups white wine
salt and pepper
12 black olives, stoned

Dice the aubergine and sprinkle with salt. Leave to stand for 30 minutes. Rinse and dry. Meanwhile, heat the oil in a flameproof casserole and brown the veal all over. Remove with a slotted spoon. Place the aubergine, onions and peppers in the casserole and sauté gently for 5 minutes. Add the tomatoes and marjoram, cover and simmer for 5 minutes. Return the meat to the casserole, pour in the wine and mix well. Season, cover and cook in a moderate oven (160°C, 325°F, Gas Mark 3) for 1 hour, adding a little more liquid (wine or water) if necessary. Add the olives and return to the oven to heat through.

Serves 6

Blanquette de veau

METRIC/IMPERIAL/AMERICAN
1 kg/2 lb/2 lb pie veal, cubed
2 medium onions, chopped, or 12 button onions
100 g/4 oz/¼ lb baby carrots
bouquet garni
½ teaspoon dried thyme
2 bay leaves
salt and pepper
25 g/1 oz/2 tablespoons butter
25 g/1 oz/¼ cup flour
2 egg yolks
5 tablespoons/5 tablespoons/6 tablespoons cream
GARNISH:
lemon wedges
bacon rolls

Place the meat, onions, carrots, bouquet garni and herbs in a saucepan with just enough water to cover. Season. Bring to the boil and skim well. Cover and simmer gently for 1½ hours. Remove the pan from the heat and discard the bouquet garni and bay leaves.

Blend the butter into the flour to form a smooth paste and whisk this, a piece at a time, into the stew. Stir over gentle heat until thickened.

Beat together the egg yolks and cream and pour into the stew. Heat through but do not boil. Serve garnished with lemon wedges and grilled bacon rolls.

Serves 4–6

Osso buco

METRIC/IMPERIAL/AMERICAN
1.25 kg/2½ lb/2½ lb shin of veal
4 carrots, grated
2 onions, finely chopped
1 stick celery, finely chopped
5 tablespoons/5 tablespoons/6 tablespoons olive oil
1 (396-g/14-oz/14-oz) can tomatoes
bouquet garni
1 fresh basil sprig, chopped, or ½ teaspoon dried basil
3 sage leaves
salt and pepper
flour for coating
300 ml/½ pint/1¼ cups dry white wine or chicken stock
grated rind of ½ lemon mixed with 1 tablespoon chopped
    parsley and 1 crushed clove garlic, to garnish

Ask your butcher to saw the veal into 5-cm/2-inch pieces. Sauté the carrots, onions and celery in 2 tablespoons/2 tablespoons/3 tablespoons oil until beginning to brown. Add the tomatoes, and herbs. Cover and simmer. Coat the veal with seasoned flour and brown gently in the remaining oil. Add to the vegetable mixture. Drain off any excess fat from the meat pan and pour in the wine or stock. Bring to the boil, stirring, then add to the casserole. Adjust seasoning, cover and simmer gently for 1½–2 hours. Discard the bouquet garni and sage leaves. Sprinkle the garnish over the meat. Serve with rice or buttered noodles.

Serves 4–6

Veal aux champignons

METRIC/IMPERIAL/AMERICAN
1 kg/2 lb/2 lb breast of veal
50 g/2 oz/¼ cup butter
2 tablespoons/2 tablespoons/3 tablespoons oil
4 shallots, finely chopped
salt and pepper
2 tablespoons/2 tablespoons/3 tablespoons lemon juice
450 ml/¾ pint/2 cups chicken stock
0.5 kg/1 lb/1 lb button mushrooms
25 g/1 oz/¼ cup flour
150 ml/¼ pint/⅔ cup double cream
parsley sprigs and slices of lemon to garnish

Cut the meat into slices. Heat half the butter with the oil in a flameproof casserole and brown the meat gently. Add the shallots and sauté until soft. Season well and pour in the lemon juice and stock. Cover and place in a moderate oven (160°C, 325°F, Gas Mark 3) for 1 hour. Add the mushrooms and return to the oven for a further 45 minutes or until the meat is tender.

Melt the remaining butter in a saucepan and stir in the flour. Off the heat, strain in 300 ml/½ pint/1¼ cups of the cooking liquid. Return to the heat and bring to the boil, stirring continuously. Remove from the heat again and add the cream. Heat through but do not allow to boil. Pour the sauce over the veal and mushrooms and garnish with parsley and lemon slices.

Serves 4–6

Offal casseroles

Offal, which is very nutritious, easily digestible and generally cheap, is often neglected when it comes to casserole dishes. Sweetbreads, tripe, hearts, kidneys, oxtail and liver all make delicious casseroles. Ideally offal should be cooked on the same day it is purchased. Sweetbreads, kidneys and liver do not require the long, slow cooking generally associated with casserole dishes.

Braised sweetbreads

METRIC/IMPERIAL/AMERICAN
0.5 kg/1 lb/1 lb calves' or lambs' sweetbreads
4 rashers streaky bacon, chopped
1 onion, sliced
1 carrot, sliced
2 sticks celery, sliced
1 clove garlic, crushed
25 g/1 oz/2 tablespoons butter
1 tablespoon flour
450 ml/$\frac{3}{4}$ pint/2 cups chicken stock
salt and pepper
chopped parsley to garnish

Soak the sweetbreads in cold water for about 4 hours, changing the water several times. Drain and place in a saucepan. Cover with cold water and bring to the boil. Take out the sweetbreads and rinse under cold water. Remove the membrane and black veins. Wrap in a cloth and leave to cool between 2 plates, lightly weighted.

Place the sweetbreads in a casserole in a single layer. Gently sauté the bacon, onion, carrot, celery and garlic in the butter for 5 minutes, then remove and place on top of the sweetbreads.

Sprinkle the flour into the fat and cook for 1 minute, stirring. Stir in the stock and bring to the boil. Season and pour into the casserole. Cover and cook in a moderate oven (160°C, 325°F, Gas Mark 3) for 45 minutes. Garnish.

Serves 4

Tripe with onions

METRIC/IMPERIAL/AMERICAN
0.5 kg/1 lb/1 lb dressed tripe
0.5 kg/1 lb/1 lb onions, sliced
300 ml/½ pint/1¼ cups chicken stock
150 ml/¼ pint/⅔ cup white wine
1 bay leaf
bouquet garni
salt and pepper
40 g/1½ oz/3 tablespoons butter
40 g/1½ oz/6 tablespoons flour
150 ml/¼ pint/⅔ cup milk or cream
chopped parsley to garnish

Cut the tripe into 2.5-cm/1-inch pieces and place in the bottom of a casserole. Cover with the onions and pour in the stock and wine. Add the bay leaf and bouquet garni and season to taste. Cover and place in a cool oven (150°C, 300°F, Gas Mark 2) for about 3 hours or until the tripe is tender. Strain off the liquid and reserve. Discard the bay leaf and bouquet garni. Keep the tripe warm in a dish.

Melt the butter in a saucepan and add the flour. Cook, stirring, for 1 minute. Remove from the heat and gradually add the reserved cooking liquid. Return to the heat and bring to the boil, stirring continuously. Add the milk or cream and heat through, but do not boil if using cream. Pour over the tripe.

Serves 4

Casserole of stuffed hearts

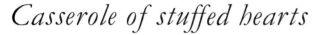

METRIC/IMPERIAL/AMERICAN
4 lambs' hearts
3 tablespoons/3 tablespoons/¼ cup oil
2 tablespoons/2 tablespoons/3 tablespoons flour
600 ml/1 pint/2½ cups beef stock
2 onions, sliced
4 carrots, sliced
bouquet garni
watercress to garnish
STUFFING:
1 onion, finely chopped
1 stick celery, finely chopped
grated rind of ½ orange
2 walnuts, chopped
40 g/1½ oz/¾ cup fresh breadcrumbs
1 tablespoon melted butter
½ beaten egg
salt and pepper

Prepare the hearts. Mix all the stuffing ingredients and fill the hearts with the mixture. Sew up.

Heat the oil in a pan, add the hearts and brown. Place in the casserole. Sprinkle the flour into the fat and cook, stirring, for 1 minute. Remove from the heat and add the stock. Bring to the boil, stirring. Season and pour over the hearts. Add the onions, carrots and bouquet garni. Cover and place in a moderate oven (160°C, 325°F, Gas Mark 3) for 3 hours. Garnish.

Serves 4

Casseroled kidneys

METRIC/IMPERIAL/AMERICAN
6 lambs' kidneys
salt and pepper
2 tablespoons/2 tablespoons/3 tablespoons flour
50 g/2 oz/¼ cup butter
8 chipolatas, halved, or 16 cocktail sausages
3 onions, sliced
1 (396-g/14-oz/14-oz) can tomatoes
2 teaspoons Worcestershire sauce
8 rashers streaky bacon
fried croûtons and 1 tablespoon chopped parsley to
    garnish

Wash, skin, halve and core the kidneys. Coat in seasoned flour. Melt the butter in a saucepan or deep frying pan and sauté the kidneys quickly to seal. Remove.

Lower the heat and place the chipolatas in the pan. Cook gently until golden brown all over. Remove and reserve. Lastly, sauté the onions until softened.

Drain off any excess fat and return the chipolatas and the kidneys with their juices to the pan. Add the tomatoes and Worcestershire sauce. Cover and simmer very gently for 15 minutes.

Meanwhile, halve the bacon rashers and roll up. Place under a hot grill until cooked through. Cut the slices of bread into triangles for croûtons and fry in oil. Serve the kidneys and chipolatas with the bacon rolls and garnish.

Serves 4

Lambs' kidneys in Madeira

METRIC/IMPERIAL/AMERICAN
10 lambs' kidneys
50 g/2 oz/¼ cup butter
1 onion, chopped
1 tablespoon flour
150 ml/¼ pint/⅔ cup Madeira or medium sweet sherry
150 ml/¼ pint/⅔ cup chicken stock
225 g/8 oz/2 cups mushrooms, halved
salt and pepper
chopped green pepper to garnish

Wash, skin and core the kidneys and cut them into quarters. Melt the butter in a saucepan or deep frying pan and sauté the onion until softened. Remove and reserve. Add the kidneys to the pan and seal them quickly on all sides.

Sprinkle in the flour and add the Madeira and stock. Bring to the boil, stirring continuously, then lower the heat. Return the onion to the pan and add the mushrooms. Season to taste, cover and simmer gently for 10 minutes. Do not overcook the kidneys or they will toughen. Garnish with chopped green pepper and serve with French bread or boiled rice.

Serves 4

Calves' kidneys in white wine

METRIC/IMPERIAL/AMERICAN
3 calves' kidneys
75 g/3 oz/6 tablespoons butter
8 shallots
3 tablespoons/3 tablespoons/$\frac{1}{4}$ cup flour
150 ml/$\frac{1}{4}$ pint/$\frac{2}{3}$ cup white wine
300 ml/$\frac{1}{2}$ pint/$1\frac{1}{4}$ cups chicken stock
1 thyme sprig, finely chopped
2 cloves garlic, crushed
pinch nutmeg
salt and pepper

Remove the fat, skin and core from the kidneys and cut them into pieces the size of a walnut. Melt half the butter in a large pan and quickly brown the kidneys all over. Remove the kidneys and keep warm.

Heat the remaining butter in the pan and gently sauté the shallots until soft. Sprinkle in the flour and cook for 2 minutes, stirring. Pour in the wine and stock gradually. Stir continuously until the sauce begins to thicken, then add the thyme, garlic, nutmeg, salt and pepper.

Replace the kidneys, cover and simmer gently for 15 minutes. Do not overcook or the kidneys will become tough.

Serve with boiled rice or sautéed diced potatoes.

Serves 4

Oxtail hotpot

METRIC/IMPERIAL/AMERICAN
2 oxtails, cut into joints
salt and pepper
2 tablespoons/2 tablespoons/3 tablespoons flour
50 g/2 oz/$\frac{1}{4}$ cup beef dripping
3 large onions, sliced
225 g/8 oz/$1\frac{1}{2}$ cups carrots, sliced
600 ml/1 pint/$2\frac{1}{2}$ cups beef stock
bouquet garni
1 bay leaf
225 g/8 oz/1 cup tomatoes, peeled and chopped
2 sticks celery, chopped
juice of $\frac{1}{2}$ lemon

Coat the oxtail in seasoned flour. Melt the dripping in a saucepan and sauté the oxtail until golden. Transfer the oxtail to a deep casserole. Sauté the onions and carrots in the fat remaining, then add to the oxtail. Pour in the stock and add the bouquet garni and bay leaf. Cover and place in a cool oven (150°C, 300°F, Gas Mark 2) for $2\frac{1}{2}$ hours. Strain off the liquid into a large bowl and leave to cool. Keep the meat, herbs and vegetables in the refrigerator. When the liquid is cold, lift off the fat. Return the oxtail, herbs and vegetables to the casserole. Add the tomatoes, celery and lemon juice. Bring the skimmed sauce to the boil, then pour over the meat. Adjust seasoning, cover and return to the oven for a further $1\frac{1}{2}$ hours.

Serves 6

Liver à l'orange

METRIC/IMPERIAL/AMERICAN
2 oranges
2 tablespoons/2 tablespoons/3 tablespoons oil
1 onion, chopped
1 clove garlic, crushed
0.5 kg/1 lb/1 lb lambs' liver
salt and pepper
2 tablespoons/2 tablespoons/3 tablespoons flour
100 g/4 oz/1 cup mushrooms, whole
1 (64-g/2¼-oz/2¼-oz) packet instant potato
chopped parsley to garnish

Thinly peel one of the oranges. Cut this into thin strips and blanch in 300 ml/½ pint/1¼ cups boiling water for 1 minute. Drain, reserving the peel and the water. Squeeze the juice from both oranges. Heat the oil in a flameproof casserole and sauté the onion and garlic. Slice the liver and coat in seasoned flour. Sauté gently in the oil in the pan. Add the mushrooms and the orange juice made up to 300 ml/½ pint/1¼ cups with the reserved blanching water. Season and bring to the boil, stirring. Cover and lower the heat. Simmer gently for 20 minutes.

Make up the potato and pipe a border around the edge of a dish. Arrange the liver in the centre and garnish with blanched peel and parsley.

Serves 4

Liver à l'italienne

METRIC/IMPERIAL/AMERICAN
0.5 kg/1 lb/1 lb lambs' liver
salt and pepper
25 g/1 oz/¼ cup flour
40 g/1½ oz/3 tablespoons butter
4 onions, sliced into rings
4 tomatoes, peeled and sliced
300 ml/½ pint/1¼ cups chicken stock
2 tablespoons/2 tablespoons/3 tablespoons tomato purée
dash Tabasco sauce
1 clove garlic, crushed
½ teaspoon dried oregano
½ teaspoon dried thyme
150 ml/¼ pint/⅔ cup double cream
chopped red pepper to garnish

Cut the liver into fingers and coat in seasoned flour. Heat the butter in a flameproof casserole and gently sauté the onions until softened. Remove.

Sauté the liver in the butter until lightly browned all over. Return the onions to the pan and add the tomatoes, stock, tomato purée, Tabasco sauce, garlic and herbs. Bring to the boil then cover and place in a moderate oven (180°C, 350°F, Gas Mark 4) for 30 minutes. Stir in the cream and heat through without boiling. Adjust seasoning if necessary. Serve with spaghetti and garnish with chopped red pepper.

Serves 4

Poultry and game casseroles

With the rearing and storage methods of today, most poultry (chicken in particular) benefits from being casseroled rather than roasted. Whole birds or joints may be cooked in a casserole. Many game birds, particularly older ones, are best braised. When using frozen poultry and game it must first be allowed to thaw.

Celebration duck

METRIC/IMPERIAL/AMERICAN
1 (1.75-kg/4-lb/4-lb) duckling
salt and pepper
25 g/1 oz/$\frac{1}{4}$ cup flour
25 g/1 oz/2 tablespoons butter
2 onions, sliced
150 ml/$\frac{1}{4}$ pint/$\frac{2}{3}$ cup medium-sweet sherry
150 ml/$\frac{1}{4}$ pint/$\frac{2}{3}$ cup chicken stock
1 clove garlic, crushed
2 tablespoons/2 tablespoons/3 tablespoons tomato purée
2 teaspoons chilli sauce
2 tablespoons/2 tablespoons/3 tablespoons chopped
   parsley
225 g/8 oz/$\frac{1}{2}$ lb fresh red cherries, stoned, or
   1 (227-g/8-oz/8-oz) can red cherries, drained and stoned
watercress to garnish

Divide the duckling into 4 joints and cut away any excess fat. Coat in seasoned flour. Melt the butter in a flameproof casserole and brown the duck pieces on all sides. Add the onions and cook until softened, then drain off all fat. Mix together the remaining ingredients, except the cherries, and pour over the duck. Cover and place in a moderate oven (180°C, 350°F, Gas Mark 4) for 45–60 minutes. Garnish with cherries and watercress.

Serves 4

Duckling with grapes

METRIC/IMPERIAL/AMERICAN
25 g/1 oz/2 tablespoons butter
1 (1.75-kg/4-lb/4-lb) duckling, trussed
2 onions, sliced
1 clove garlic, crushed
1–2 tablespoons/1–2 tablespoons/1–3 tablespoons flour
150 ml/¼ pint/⅔ cup dry white wine
300 ml/½ pint/1¼ cups chicken stock
salt and pepper
bouquet garni
GARNISH:
225 g/8 oz/½ lb black grapes
watercress

Melt the butter in a large flameproof casserole and brown the duckling on all sides. Remove the duckling and sauté the onions and garlic in the fat remaining in the casserole. Pour off most of the excess fat, leaving about 2 tablespoons/2 tablespoons/3 tablespoons. Sprinkle in the flour and cook, stirring, for 1 minute. Gradually add the wine and stock and bring to the boil, stirring continuously. Season to taste, return the duck to the casserole and add the bouquet garni. Cover and cook in a moderate oven (180°C, 350°F, Gas Mark 4) for 1½–2 hours.

Remove the duckling from the casserole and keep hot. Discard the bouquet garni and skim all fat from the sauce.

To serve, place the duckling on a serving platter. Arrange the grapes around the duck and serve the sauce separately. Garnish.

Serves 4–6

Poule au pot

METRIC/IMPERIAL/AMERICAN
1 (1.5-kg/3½-lb/3½-lb) boiling chicken with giblets
600 ml/1 pint/2½ cups water
salt and freshly ground black pepper
3 onions
50 g/2 oz/¼ cup butter
6 carrots, thickly sliced
3 sticks celery, chopped
2 turnips, quartered
2 bay leaves
25 g/1 oz/¼ cup flour

Place the giblets in a saucepan with the water and 1 teaspoon salt. Bring to the boil then cover and simmer for 30 minutes. Meanwhile, place a large onion inside the chicken and truss as for roasting a chicken. Melt half the butter in a large flameproof casserole and brown the chicken all over. Pour off all fat from the casserole. Quarter the remaining onions and arrange around the chicken with the other vegetables and bay leaves. Strain in the giblet stock and season with pepper. Cover and place in a moderate oven (160°C, 325°F, Gas Mark 3) for 2–2½ hours or until tender. Arrange the chicken and vegetables on a large platter. Keep warm. Skim any fat off the sauce. Blend together the remaining butter and the flour to form a paste. Add to the sauce, a little at a time, and stir over a gentle heat until thickened. Do not boil. Adjust seasoning and serve the sauce separately.

Serves 4–6

Curried chicken

METRIC/IMPERIAL/AMERICAN
8–12 chicken drumsticks, skinned
150 ml/¼ pint/⅔ cup natural yogurt
20 coriander seeds
2 tablespoons/2 tablespoons/3 tablespoons flour
1 tablespoon curry powder
1 teaspoon ground ginger
½ teaspoon ground turmeric
50 g/2 oz/¼ cup butter
2 onions, sliced
2 cloves garlic, crushed
2 sticks celery, chopped
4 tomatoes, peeled and chopped
300 ml/½ pint/1¼ cups chicken stock
juice of ½ lemon
salt and pepper

Marinate the chicken for 2–4 hours in the yogurt mixed with the coriander seeds. Dry the drumsticks. Reserve the marinade. Coat the chicken with the flour mixed with the curry powder, ginger and turmeric, then sauté lightly in the butter in a flameproof casserole. Remove. Sauté the onions, garlic and celery in the casserole until softened. Strain off any excess fat before adding the tomatoes, drumsticks, stock and lemon juice. Season. Cover and place in a moderate oven (180°C, 350°F, Gas Mark 4) for 30–45 minutes until tender. Pour the yogurt marinade over the chicken and garnish with chopped parsley.

Serves 4

Escalopes of turkey with tomatoes and herbs

METRIC/IMPERIAL/AMERICAN
4 turkey escalopes
25 g/1 oz/2 tablespoons butter
salt and pepper
2 onions, finely chopped
2 cloves garlic, crushed
2 tablespoons/2 tablespoons/3 tablespoons chopped fresh chervil
1 tablespoon chopped fresh thyme or 1 teaspoon dried thyme
1 (396-g/14-oz/14-oz) can tomatoes
chopped parsley to garnish

Turkey escalopes are cut from the breast and can now be purchased ready cut.

Melt the butter in a frying pan and sauté the turkey escalopes for 3 minutes on each side. Place in a casserole and season well. Spread with the onions, mixed with the garlic and herbs. Pour in the tomatoes with their juice and cook, uncovered, in a moderate oven (180°C, 350°F, Gas Mark 4) for 30 minutes. Garnish with chopped parsley and serve with sautéed or creamed potatoes.

Serves 4

Chicken in champagne

METRIC/IMPERIAL/AMERICAN

1 (2-kg/4½-lb/4½-lb) chicken, jointed
75 g/3 oz/6 tablespoons butter
4 shallots, finely chopped
2 tablespoons/2 tablespoons/3 tablespoons brandy
300 ml/½ pint/1¼ cups chicken stock
150 ml/¼ pint/⅔ cup champagne
bouquet garni
salt and pepper
225 g/8 oz/2 cups mushrooms, sliced
25 g/1 oz/¼ cup flour
3 tablespoons/3 tablespoons/¼ cup double cream
parsley sprig to garnish

Sauté the chicken in 50 g/2 oz/¼ cup butter in a flameproof casserole, until golden all over. Add the shallots, sauté lightly then pour in the brandy. Cover, remove from the heat and leave to infuse for 5 minutes. Add the stock, champagne and bouquet garni. Season. Cover and place in a moderate oven (180°C, 350°F, Gas Mark 4) for 30 minutes. Add the mushrooms and cook for a further 30 minutes. Transfer the chicken to a deep serving platter. Keep warm.

Blend the remaining butter and the flour together and add, piece by piece, to the sauce in the casserole. Stir over a low heat until thickened. Do not boil. Stir in the cream. Pour over the chicken and garnish with parsley.

Serves 6

Chicken chasseur

METRIC/IMPERIAL/AMERICAN

1 carrot, chopped
2 onions, chopped
25 g/1 oz/2 tablespoons bacon, diced
25 g/1 oz/2 tablespoons butter
50 g/2 oz/½ cup flour
450 ml/¾ pint/2 cups beef stock
1 tablespoon tomato purée
150 ml/¼ pint/⅔ cup white wine
salt and pepper
4 chicken joints
4 tablespoons/4 tablespoons/⅓ cup olive oil
100 g/4 oz/1 cup button mushrooms
100 g/4 oz/½ cup tomatoes, peeled and chopped
parsley sprig to garnish

Sauté the carrot, 1 onion and the bacon in the butter until the vegetables begin to brown. Stir in half the flour and cook until browning. Gradually add the stock, tomato purée and wine. Season, cover and simmer very gently for 1 hour. Strain and skim. Coat the chicken joints in the remaining flour and sauté in the oil in a flameproof casserole. Remove. Add the remaining onion to the casserole and sauté until softened. Strain off any excess fat, then add the chicken, mushrooms and tomatoes. Pour in the sauce and adjust seasoning if necessary. Cover and cook in a moderate oven (180°C, 350°F, Gas Mark 4) for 1–1½ hour. Garnish with parsley.

Serves 4

Chicken with pineapple

METRIC/IMPERIAL/AMERICAN
4 tablespoons/4 tablespoons/⅓ cup olive oil
4 chicken joints
1 green pepper, deseeded and chopped
2 sticks celery, chopped
1 onion, chopped
1 (198-g/7-oz/7-oz) can pineapple slices
1 tablespoon soy sauce
1 tablespoon lemon juice
1 tablespoon tomato purée
salt and pepper
watercress to garnish

Heat the oil in a large frying pan and fry the chicken joints until golden. Transfer to a casserole. Add the pepper, celery and onion to the pan and sauté until softened. Transfer to the casserole. Add the syrup from the pineapple with the soy sauce, lemon juice and tomato purée to the chicken and vegetables. Season to taste. Cover and cook in a moderate oven (180°C, 350°F, Gas Mark 4) for 45 minutes. Arrange the halved pineapple slices on top of the chicken and return, uncovered, to the oven for a final 15 minutes. Garnish with watercress and serve with boiled rice and mushrooms.

Serves 4

Coq au vin

METRIC/IMPERIAL/AMERICAN
1 (2-kg/4½-lb/4½-lb) chicken with giblets, jointed
salt and pepper
100 g/4 oz/½ cup bacon, chopped
20 button onions
75 g/3 oz/6 tablespoons butter
4 tablespoons/4 tablespoons/⅓ cup brandy
450 ml/¾ pint/2 cups red wine
225 g/8 oz/½ lb mushrooms, sliced
2 cloves garlic, crushed
2 teaspoons soft brown sugar
bouquet garni
pinch ground nutmeg
40 g/1½ oz/6 tablespoons flour
chopped parsley to garnish

Simmer the giblets for 30 minutes in salted water. In a flameproof casserole, sauté the bacon and onions in half the butter until golden. Remove. Add the chicken joints and brown. Pour the brandy, flaming, over the chicken. Return the bacon and onions and add the wine, 150 ml/¼ pint/⅔ cup strained giblet stock, mushrooms, garlic, sugar, herbs, nutmeg and pepper. Bring to the boil, cover and cook in a moderate oven (180°C, 350°F, Gas Mark 4) for 1 hour.

Remove the chicken pieces and keep warm. Blend together the butter and flour and whisk, little by little, into the sauce. Heat through until thickened. Return chicken and garnish.

Serves 6

Chicken Marengo

METRIC/IMPERIAL/AMERICAN
1 (2-kg/4½-lb/4½-lb) chicken or 6 chicken joints
50 g/2 oz/¼ cup butter
2 tablespoons/2 tablespoons/3 tablespoons olive oil
2 onions, sliced
2 carrots, sliced
1 clove garlic, crushed
1½ tablespoons/1½ tablespoons/2 tablespoons flour
300 ml/½ pint/1¼ cups chicken stock
6 tablespoons/6 tablespoons/½ cup Marsala or sherry
225 g/8 oz/2 cups mushrooms, sliced
225 g/8 oz/1 cup tomatoes, sliced
salt and freshly ground black pepper
1 tablespoon brandy (optional)
chopped parsley to garnish

Joint the chicken if using a whole bird. Heat the butter and oil in a flameproof casserole and sauté the chicken pieces until golden all over. Remove. Sauté the onions, carrots and garlic in the casserole until softened. Sprinkle in the flour and cook, stirring, for 1 minute. Gradually stir in the stock and Marsala and bring to the boil. Reduce the heat. Return the chicken to the casserole and add the mushrooms and tomatoes. Season, cover and place in a moderate oven (180°C, 350°F, Gas Mark 4) for 1–1½ hours. Stir the brandy into the sauce just before serving. Garnish with parsley.

Serves 6

Jugged hare

METRIC/IMPERIAL/AMERICAN
1 hare, jointed
175 g/6 oz/¾ cup streaky bacon, chopped
50 g/2 oz/¼ cup butter
2 onions, sliced
25 g/1 oz/¼ cup flour
750 ml/1¼ pints/3 cups stock or stock and red wine
bouquet garni
grated rind of ½ lemon
1 tablespoon redcurrant jelly

Reserve hare's blood and add a few drops of vinegar to it. Sauté the bacon and hare joints in the butter in a flameproof casserole. Remove. Sauté the onions, then sprinkle in the flour and cook, stirring. Blend in the stock and wine. Bring to the boil, stirring. Add the hare, bacon, bouquet garni and lemon rind. Season. Cover and place in a moderate oven (180°C, 350°F, Gas Mark 4) for 3 hours. Meanwhile, prepare stuffing balls. Sauté 1 chopped onion, 2 chopped sticks celery and 1 chopped cooking apple in 25 g/1 oz/2 tablespoons butter. Add 100 g/4 oz/2 cups white breadcrumbs and bind with 1 beaten egg. Season. Roll into balls and bake in the oven for 30 minutes.

Discard bouquet garni and stir the redcurrant jelly into the casserole. Blend a little sauce into the blood, then stir into the casserole. Heat, garnish and serve with stuffing balls.

Serves 6

Rabbit fricassée

METRIC/IMPERIAL/AMERICAN
1 (1.5-kg/3-lb/3-lb) rabbit, jointed
2 large onions, sliced
2 carrots, sliced
2 sticks celery, chopped
bouquet garni
450 ml/¾ pint/2 cups chicken stock
150 ml/¼ pint/⅔ cup white wine
salt and pepper
100 g/4 oz/1 cup button mushrooms
75 g/3 oz/6 tablespoons butter
100 g/4 oz/¼ lb button onions
25 g/1 oz/¼ cup flour
2 egg yolks
150 ml/¼ pint/⅔ cup double cream
chopped parsley and triangles of fried bread to garnish

Place the rabbit in a casserole with the onions, carrots, celery, bouquet garni, stock, wine and seasoning. Cover and cook in a moderate oven (180°C, 350°F, Gas Mark 4) for 1½ hours. Remove the rabbit and keep warm. Reserve the cooking liquor. Sauté the mushrooms in half the butter and cook the button onions in boiling salted water for 5 minutes. Melt the remaining butter and stir in the flour. Blend in 450 ml/¾ pint/2 cups of the strained rabbit liquid. Bring to the boil, stirring continuously. Add the mushrooms and onions. Stir in the egg yolks beaten with the cream. Warm and pour over the rabbit.

Serves 4

Partridges with cabbage

METRIC/IMPERIAL/AMERICAN
1 green, white or red cabbage, quartered
salt
25 g/1 oz/2 tablespoons bacon fat or butter
2 partridges, plucked, drawn and trussed
8 chipolatas
2 onions, chopped
6 rashers streaky bacon, chopped
½ teaspoon ground cloves
freshly ground black pepper
300 ml/½ pint/1¼ cups red wine or wine and stock
watercress to garnish

Blanch the cabbage for 5 minutes in boiling salted water. Drain.
    Melt the bacon fat or butter in a large frying pan and brown the partridges and chipolatas all over. Remove. Sauté the onions in the fat remaining in the pan. Sprinkle the bacon in the base of a casserole.
    Shred the cabbage and mix with the onion and ground cloves. Spread half the cabbage mixture over the bacon, season with pepper and place the partridges and chipolatas on top. Cover with the remaining cabbage, season with more pepper and pour over the wine. Cover and cook in a moderate oven (160°C, 325°F, Gas Mark 3) for about 1½ hours or until the birds are tender. The exact time will depend on the age of the birds. Garnish with watercress.

Serves 4

Pigeons in tomato sauce

METRIC/IMPERIAL/AMERICAN
4 pigeons
175 g/6 oz/6 oz belly of pork, cubed
25 g/1 oz/2 tablespoons butter
225 g/8 oz/½ lb button onions
25 g/1 oz/¼ cup flour
300 ml/½ pint/1¼ cups white wine
1 (396-g/14-oz/14-oz) can tomatoes
2 cloves garlic, crushed
bouquet garni
1 teaspoon Worcestershire sauce
225 g/8 oz/½ lb button mushrooms
1 tablespoon chopped parsley

Wash the pigeons thoroughly, discarding the giblets, and dry
well. Sauté the pork in the butter until golden. Transfer to a
large casserole. Sauté the onions gently in the fat in the pan then
transfer to the casserole. Add the pigeons to the pan and
carefully brown on all sides. Place on the pork and onions. Stir
the flour into the fat in the pan and cook for 1 minute. Add the
wine and tomatoes and bring to the boil, stirring continuously.
Add the garlic, bouquet garni and Worcestershire sauce. Pour
over the pigeons, cover and place in a moderate oven (180°C,
350°F, Gas Mark 4) for 1½ hours. Add the mushrooms and
parsley and return to the oven for a further 30 minutes. Remove
the bouquet garni.

Serves 4

Venison stew

METRIC/IMPERIAL/AMERICAN
1 kg/2 lb/2 lb shoulder of venison, cubed
300 ml/½ pint/1¼ cups red wine
1 large carrot, sliced
1 onion, sliced
2 cloves garlic
2 tablespoons/2 tablespoons/3 tablespoons olive oil
bouquet garni
salt and pepper
25 g/1 oz/2 tablespoons butter
225 g/8 oz/1 cup bacon, diced
225 g/8 oz/½ lb button onions
2 tablespoons/2 tablespoons/3 tablespoons flour
1 bay leaf

Place the meat in a shallow dish. Mix together the wine, carrot,
onion, garlic, oil, bouquet garni and seasoning. Pour over the
meat. Marinate for 12 hours. Dry the meat. Reserve the
marinade. Heat the butter in a flameproof casserole and sauté
the bacon and onions lightly. Remove. Add the meat to the
casserole and brown over a high heat. Lower the heat and
sprinkle in the flour. Mix well and cook for 1 minute. Strain the
marinade liquid (discarding the vegetables) over the meat,
adding just enough water to cover. Bring to the boil, stirring
continuously, then lower the heat. Add the bacon, onions and
bay leaf. Season. Cover and place in a moderate oven (160°C,
325°F, Gas Mark 3) for 1½–2 hours. Remove the bay leaf.

Serves 4–6

Casseroled grouse

METRIC/IMPERIAL/AMERICAN

4 mature grouse, trussed
salt and pepper
25 g/1 oz/2 tablespoons butter
2 tablespoons/2 tablespoons/3 tablespoons olive oil
6 shallots, roughly chopped
2 sticks celery, chopped
2 cloves garlic, crushed
1–1½ tablespoons flour
300 ml/½ pint/1¼ cups beef stock
300 ml/½ pint/1¼ cups red wine
8 juniper berries, crushed
2 teaspoons chopped fresh marjoram or 1 teaspoon dried
    marjoram
225 g/8 oz/½ lb button mushrooms

Season the grouse inside and out, and brown all over in the butter and oil in a large flameproof casserole. Remove. Sauté the shallots, celery and garlic in the fat remaining in the pan, then sprinkle in enough flour to soak up the fat. Cook until the flour is beginning to brown then carefully blend in the stock and wine. Bring to the boil, stirring constantly, then return the grouse to the casserole and add the juniper berries and marjoram. Adjust seasoning, cover and cook in a moderate oven (180°C, 350°F, Gas Mark 4) for 1 hour.

Add the mushrooms and continue cooking for a further 30 minutes or until the birds are tender.

Serves 4

Faisan à la normande

METRIC/IMPERIAL/AMERICAN

1 pheasant, with giblets, jointed
bouquet garni
salt and pepper
4 tablespoons/4 tablespoons/⅓ cup oil
2 onions, sliced
2 sticks celery, chopped
2 tablespoons/2 tablespoons/3 tablespoons brandy
300 ml/½ pint/1¼ cups dry cider
1 bay leaf
225 g/8 oz/½ lb cooking apples
2 egg yolks
150 ml/¼ pint/⅔ cup single cream
finely chopped walnuts to garnish

Place giblets and bouquet garni in a pan with 300 ml/½ pint/1¼ cups salted water. Bring to the boil. Cover and simmer for 30 minutes then boil down by half. Meanwhile, coat pheasant in seasoned flour and brown in the oil. Remove. Sauté the onions and celery for 5 minutes. Return the pheasant to the casserole.

Pour brandy, flaming, over pheasant. Strain in giblet stock and add cider and bay leaf. Bring to the boil, cover and place in a moderate oven (180°C, 350°F, Gas Mark 4) for 30 minutes.

Peel, core and slice apples. Add to casserole and return to the oven for a further 30 minutes. Remove pheasant. Stir yolks beaten with the cream into the sauce. Warm through then return the pheasant and garnish.

Serves 4

Vegetable and dessert casseroles

Vegetables cooked in a small amount of liquid in a covered container in the oven are infinitely better than when boiled in too much water in a pan. The vegetable recipes in this section may be served as a dish on their own for a light meal or as an accompaniment to any main course dish.

Included in this section are recipes for fruit which also benefits from being cooked in the oven – soft fruits in particular.

Leeks à la portugaise

METRIC/IMPERIAL/AMERICAN
1 kg/2 lb/2 lb leeks
salt
1 onion, chopped
2 tablespoons/2 tablespoons/3 tablespoons oil
0.5 kg/1 lb/2 cups tomatoes, peeled and chopped
1 clove garlic, crushed
2 tablespoons/2 tablespoons/3 tablespoons chopped
  parsley
2 tablespoons/2 tablespoons/3 tablespoons dry white
  wine
freshly ground black pepper
chopped parsley to garnish

Cut the roots and leaves off the leeks. Wash thoroughly and blanch in boiling salted water for 5 minutes. Drain well and arrange in an ovenproof dish.

Meanwhile, sauté the onion in the oil until softened, then add the remaining ingredients and cook, covered, for 5 minutes. Pour this sauce over the leeks, cover and cook in a moderate oven (180°C, 350°F, Gas Mark 4) for 45–55 minutes. Garnish with chopped parsley. Delicious hot with fish or cold as a starter.

Serves 4–6

Mushrooms and courgettes in garlic butter

METRIC/IMPERIAL/AMERICAN
225 g/8 oz/½ lb flat mushrooms
225 g/8 oz/½ lb courgettes
salt
100 g/4 oz/½ cup butter
3 cloves garlic, crushed
2 tablespoons/2 tablespoons/3 tablespoons chopped
    parsley
grated rind of 1 lemon

Wipe the mushrooms carefully. Cut the courgettes into 5-mm/
¼-inch slices and blanch for 1 minute in boiling salted water.
Drain well and pat dry.

Arrange the mushrooms and courgettes in the bottom of an
ovenproof dish. Melt the butter in a saucepan and add the
garlic. Pour the garlic butter over the mushrooms and
courgettes and bake, uncovered, in a moderately hot oven
(200°C, 400°F, Gas Mark 6) for 15 minutes. Sprinkle the parsley
mixed with the lemon rind over the dish and return to the oven
for a further 5 minutes. Spoon the garlic butter over the
vegetables when serving. This dish is delicious with roast or
grilled meat, or alone as a starter.

Serves 4

Potatoes lyonnaise

METRIC/IMPERIAL/AMERICAN
0.75 kg/1½ lb/1½ lb potatoes
salt
100 g/4 oz/½ cup butter
1 clove garlic, crushed
225 g/8 oz/2 cups onions, chopped
1–2 tablespoons/1–2 tablespoons/2–3 tablespoons milk
freshly ground black pepper
3 tablespoons/3 tablespoons/¼ cup chopped fresh parsley
    or 25 g/1 oz/¼ cup Parmesan cheese, grated
GARNISH:
slices of tomato
parsley sprigs

Peel the potatoes and boil them until just tender in salted water.
Meanwhile, melt three-quarters of the butter in a frying pan
and sauté the garlic and onions until softened.

Drain the potatoes and mash. Mix in all the contents of the
frying pan and enough milk to bind without making the
mixture too wet. Season to taste with salt and freshly ground
black pepper. Either chopped parsley or grated cheese can be
added according to taste.

Spoon the potato mixture into greased individual ovenproof
dishes and dot with the remaining butter. Bake, uncovered, in a
moderately hot oven (200°C, 400°F, Gas Mark 6) for 20
minutes. Garnish each dish with a slice of tomato and parsley.

This dish is particularly tasty with fish.

Serves 4

Macedoine à la française

METRIC/IMPERIAL/AMERICAN
100 g/4 oz/½ cup streaky bacon, chopped
12 button onions, whole
225 g/8 oz/½ lb young carrots
150 ml/¼ pint/⅔ cup chicken stock
50 g/2 oz/¼ cup butter
1 tablespoon sugar
salt
0.5 kg/1 lb/1 lb fresh peas, shelled or 225 g/8 oz/½ lb
    frozen peas
1 (56-g/2-oz/2-oz) can anchovy fillets, halved
chopped parsley to garnish

Gently sauté the bacon in a saucepan or flameproof casserole until the fat runs. Add the onions and sauté in the bacon fat until beginning to colour. Remove the onions and add the carrots (whole if they are small; otherwise slice), stock, butter, sugar and salt to taste. Bring to the boil, cover and simmer for 20 minutes. Add the peas after 10 minutes if using fresh. After 20 minutes, uncover and raise the heat. Add frozen peas at this stage. Cook until the stock has evaporated and the vegetables and bacon are coated in a buttery glaze. Arrange the anchovy fillets in a criss-cross pattern on top of the vegetables and place the reserved onions in between. Reheat for 5 minutes. This dish is excellent served with a beef casserole.

Serves 4

Cauliflower cheese with bacon and onion

METRIC/IMPERIAL/AMERICAN
1 large cauliflower, broken into florets
salt and pepper
225 g/8 oz/1 cup streaky bacon, chopped
2 onions, chopped
40 g/1½ oz/3 tablespoons butter
25 g/1 oz/¼ cup flour
300 ml/½ pint/1¼ cups milk
2 tablespoons/2 tablespoons/3 tablespoons cream
150 g/5 oz/1¼ cups Cheddar cheese, grated
nutmeg
parsley sprig to garnish

Cook the cauliflower in boiling salted water for 10 minutes. Drain well. Meanwhile, gently sauté the bacon until golden. Remove from the pan. Sauté the onions in the bacon fat and butter until softened. Add the flour and cook, stirring, for 1 minute. Gradually blend in the milk and bring to the boil, stirring continuously. Remove from the heat and add the cream and all but 1 tablespoon of the grated cheese. Stir in the reserved bacon and season with salt, pepper and nutmeg. Pour over the cauliflower in an ovenproof dish. Sprinkle with the reserved cheese. Bake in a moderately hot oven (190°C, 375°F, Gas Mark 5) for 30–40 minutes until golden and bubbling. Garnish with parsley.

Serves 4–6

Braised red cabbage

METRIC/IMPERIAL/AMERICAN
1 red cabbage
100 g/4 oz/½ cup streaky bacon, chopped
1 onion, sliced
2 cooking apples, peeled and chopped
50 g/2 oz/⅓ cup sultanas
2 cloves garlic, crushed
3 tablespoons/3 tablespoons/¼ cup wine vinegar
2 tablespoons/2 tablespoons/3 tablespoons soft brown
    sugar
150 ml/¼ pint/⅔ cup chicken stock
grated rind of ½ lemon
salt and freshly ground black pepper
pinch nutmeg
25 g/1 oz/2 tablespoons butter

Remove the coarse outer leaves from the cabbage, quarter it, remove the central core and shred the leaves.

Place a flameproof casserole over a low heat and add the bacon. Sauté gently until the fat runs then turn up the heat and fry until crisp. Lower the heat, add the shredded cabbage and mix well. Cover and braise gently for 5 minutes.

Add the onion, apple, sultanas, garlic, wine vinegar, sugar, stock and lemon rind. Season to taste with salt, pepper and nutmeg. Mix all the ingredients thoroughly, then cover tightly and place in a cool oven (150°C, 300°F, Gas Mark 2) for 1½–2 hours, adding a little more stock if necessary. Dot with butter.

Serves 4

Dauphinoise potatoes

METRIC/IMPERIAL/AMERICAN
0.5 kg/1 lb/1 lb potatoes
2 cloves garlic
salt and pepper
175 g/6 oz/1½ cups Leicester cheese, grated
200 ml/⅓ pint/¾ cup single cream
mint sprig to garnish

Peel the potatoes and slice very thinly. Rub a cut clove of garlic around the inside of a shallow ovenproof dish and line the bottom of the dish with a layer of half the potato slices. Sprinkle with salt, pepper and a little crushed garlic. Cover with half the grated cheese. Repeat. Pour the cream over the top and bake in the centre of a moderate oven (180°C, 350°F, Gas Mark 4) for 45 minutes–1 hour. Garnish with mint. This dish makes a delicious accompaniment to roast lamb or beef.

Serves 4

Tomato and potato bake

METRIC/IMPERIAL/AMERICAN
2 tablespoons/2 tablespoons/3 tablespoons oil
2 medium onions, chopped
1 clove garlic, crushed
large rosemary sprig, chopped
thyme sprig, chopped
1 (396-g/14-oz/14-oz) can tomatoes
1 green pepper, deseeded and chopped
salt and pepper
0.5 kg/1 lb/1 lb potatoes, peeled and thinly sliced
100 g/4 oz/1 cup Cheddar cheese, grated
50 g/2 oz/1 cup fresh breadcrumbs
slices of tomato to garnish

Heat the oil in a saucepan and gently sauté the onions and garlic until soft but not browned. Add the herbs, tomatoes, pepper and seasoning to taste. Simmer gently, uncovered, until thick and pulpy.

Spread half the sauce in the bottom of an ovenproof casserole and cover with half the potato slices. Season and repeat.

Mix together the cheese and breadcrumbs and sprinkle over the potatoes. Bake in the centre of a moderately hot oven (190°C, 375°F, Gas Mark 5) for 1–1¼ hours or until the potatoes are cooked. Garnish with sliced tomatoes. Serve with a green salad as a light lunch or supper dish.

Serves 4

Ratatouille

METRIC/IMPERIAL/AMERICAN
3 aubergines
salt
5 tablespoons/5 tablespoons/6 tablespoons olive oil
225 g/8 oz/2 cups onions, chopped
0.5 kg/1 lb/2 cups tomatoes, peeled, quartered and
  deseeded
2 green peppers, deseeded and chopped
5 medium courgettes, sliced
2 cloves garlic, crushed
bouquet garni
2 teaspoons chopped fresh marjoram or 1 teaspoon dried
  marjoram
2 teaspoons sugar
freshly ground black pepper

Roughly chop the aubergines and sprinkle with salt. Leave to stand for 30 minutes, then rinse and dry thoroughly. Meanwhile, heat the oil in a large saucepan or flameproof casserole and gently sauté the onions until softened. Add the aubergines and all the remaining ingredients to the pan and cook gently for 40–50 minutes until all the vegetables are just cooked.

Remove the bouquet garni, adjust seasoning if necessary, and serve the ratatouille hot as an accompaniment to roast meat or cold as a starter.

Serves 6–8

Peppers stuffed with tuna

METRIC/IMPERIAL/AMERICAN
4 green peppers
1 (198-g/7-oz/7-oz) can tuna, drained
grated rind and juice of ½ lemon
6 anchovy fillets
1 tablespoon olive oil
75 g/3 oz/½ cup rice, cooked
2 tablespoons/2 tablespoons/3 tablespoons tomato purée
1 tablespoon chopped parsley
freshly ground black pepper
150 ml/¼ pint/⅔ cup chicken stock

Chop the stalk ends off the peppers and scoop out the seeds.
Finely chop any flesh attached to the stalks and discard the
stalks themselves. Blanch the pepper shells in boiling water for
5 minutes then drain, refresh in cold water and drain again by
standing them upside-down.

Mash the tuna in a bowl and mix in the chopped pepper and
lemon rind and juice. Pound the anchovies to a paste with
1 teaspoon olive oil and stir into the tuna with the rice, tomato
purée and parsley. Season with freshly ground black pepper.

Stuff the peppers with this mixture and arrange them in a
casserole which has been brushed with 1 teaspoon oil. Brush the
skins with the remaining oil, pour in the stock, cover and cook
in a moderate oven (180°C, 350°F, Gas Mark 4) for 30–40
minutes or until the peppers are tender.

Serves 4

Blackberry and yogurt pudding

METRIC/IMPERIAL/AMERICAN
0.5 kg/1 lb/1 lb large blackberries, fresh or frozen and
    thawed
2 tablespoons/2 tablespoons/3 tablespoons soft brown
    sugar
2 eggs
300 ml/½ pint/1¼ cups natural yogurt
1 teaspoon lemon juice
demerara sugar to decorate

Reserve a few blackberries to decorate and place the remaining
blackberries in a shallow ovenproof dish. Sprinkle with the
brown sugar. Beat the eggs into the yogurt with 1 teaspoon
lemon juice. Pour this mixture over the blackberries and cook,
uncovered, in a moderate oven (180°C, 350°F, Gas Mark 4) for
30–40 minutes or until the topping is firm. Sprinkle generously
with demerara sugar and decorate with reserved blackberries.

Serves 4

Baked apples in orange

METRIC/IMPERIAL/AMERICAN
4 medium cooking or crisp eating apples
juice of 1 lemon
FILLING:
25 g/1 oz/2 tablespoons butter
25 g/1 oz/¼ cup icing sugar
1 egg yolk
50 g/2 oz/½ cup ground almonds
grated rind of 1 orange

juice of 3 oranges
angelica leaves to decorate

Peel and core the apples, leaving them whole. Brush with lemon juice to prevent discoloration. Arrange upright in an ovenproof dish.

Cream together the filling ingredients and use this mixture to stuff the centres of the apples.

Pour the orange juice around the apples and bake in a moderate oven (180°C, 350°F, Gas Mark 4) for 45 minutes–1 hour, basting frequently with orange juice. The apples should be tender but still hold their shape. Decorate each apple with angelica leaves.

Serves 4

Cherry clafoutis

METRIC/IMPERIAL/AMERICAN
0.5 kg/1 lb/1 lb black cherries or 1 (425-g/15-oz/15-oz)
   can black cherries
25 g/1 oz/2 tablespoons butter
2 eggs
25 g/1 oz/¼ cup flour
pinch salt
40 g/1½ oz/3 tablespoons castor sugar
300 ml/½ pint/1¼ cups milk
few drops almond essence
1 tablespoon icing sugar

If using fresh cherries, remove the stalks and wash, stone and drain the fruit. If using canned cherries, drain thoroughly and stone. Use half the butter to grease an ovenproof dish and arrange the cherries evenly in the dish.

Beat the eggs together in a bowl, then blend in the flour sifted with the salt. Add the sugar and mix well. Stir in the milk and the almond essence. Melt the remaining butter and beat into the batter. Pour the batter over the cherries and bake just above the centre of a moderately hot oven (190°C, 375°F, Gas Mark 5) for 45 minutes–1 hour until set but still creamy. Sprinkle with icing sugar just before serving lukewarm.

Serves 4

Peaches in sherry and almond sauce

METRIC/IMPERIAL/AMERICAN
6 medium peaches or 1 (539-g/15½-oz/15½-oz) can white
   peach halves
25 g/1 oz/2 tablespoons soft brown sugar
25 g/1 oz/¼ cup flaked almonds
6 tablespoons/6 tablespoons/½ cup medium-sweet sherry

Nick the skins of the fresh peaches, put them in a basin and
cover with boiling water for 30 seconds. Remove with a slotted
spoon and cool in cold water. The skins can now be peeled off
easily.

   Halve the peaches, remove the stones and arrange the peach
halves in a casserole. Sprinkle with the sugar and a few flaked
almonds, reserving some for decoration, and pour the sherry
over.

   Cover and place in a moderate oven (160°C, 325°F, Gas Mark
4) for 20 minutes. Serve with whipped cream or ice cream.
Sprinkled with the reserved almonds.

Serves 4

Pears and plums in red wine

METRIC/IMPERIAL/AMERICAN
75 g/3 oz/3 oz lump sugar
150 ml/¼ pint/⅔ cup water
150 ml/¼ pint/⅔ cup red wine
small piece cinnamon stick
4 dessert pears
juice of 1 lemon
0.5 kg/1 lb/1 lb plums

Dissolve the sugar in the water over gentle heat. Boil until
syrupy, then add the wine and cinnamon. Simmer, covered, for
5 minutes, then strain.

   Peel the pears but leave them whole. Brush with lemon juice
to prevent discoloration, and place in an ovenproof dish. Wipe
the plums and arrange them between the pears.

   Pour the wine syrup over the fruit, cover and cook in a
moderate oven (160°C, 325°F, Gas Mark 3) for 35–45 minutes.

Serves 4

Danish rhubarb layer pudding

METRIC/IMPERIAL/AMERICAN
0.5 kg/1 lb/1 lb rhubarb
2 teaspoons ground ginger
50 g/2 oz/¼ cup castor sugar
3 tablespoons/3 tablespoons/¼ cup water
50 g/2 oz/¼ cup butter
150 g/5 oz/2½ cups fresh breadcrumbs
75 g/3 oz/6 tablespoons soft brown sugar

Trim the rhubarb, wash and chop into 2.5-cm/1-inch lengths. Mix with the ginger and castor sugar. Place in a saucepan with the water and cook over gentle heat until just softened.

Meanwhile, melt the butter in a deep frying pan and add the breadcrumbs mixed with the brown sugar. Fry until crisp but do not allow the crumbs to burn.

Arrange a layer of rhubarb in an ovenproof dish and sprinkle with a layer of fried crumbs. Repeat the layers until all the rhubarb and crumbs are used up, finishing with a layer of crumbs. Place in the centre of a moderate oven (180°C, 350°F, Gas Mark 4) for 30 minutes. Serve hot with whipped cream or ice cream. This dish can be made with gooseberries instead of rhubarb, or with a mixture of both.

Serves 4–6

Oranges with raspberries

METRIC/IMPERIAL/AMERICAN
4 oranges
0.5 kg/1 lb/1 lb raspberries
225 g/8 oz/1 cup granulated sugar
150 ml/¼ pint/⅔ cup water
2 tablespoons/2 tablespoons/3 tablespoons sherry
25 g/1 oz/2 tablespoons butter

Using a potato peeler, pare the rind from 1 orange, making sure it is free from any pith. Cut the rind into very thin strips and cook in boiling water for 2 minutes. Drain.

Remove the rind, pith and skin from all the oranges and cut across the flesh in slices. Remove any pips. Do this over a plate or bowl and reserve any orange juice. Hull the raspberries.

Arrange the orange slices and raspberries in an ovenproof dish and sprinkle the shredded orange rind over the top.

Dissolve the sugar in the water over low heat, then add the sherry, butter and any orange juice. Bring to the boil and pour over the oranges and raspberries. Place, uncovered, in a moderately hot oven (190°C, 375°F, Gas Mark 5) for 30 minutes. Serve warm with cream.

Serves 4–6